AF271546

"– HI THOMAS, GOT AN IDEA,
MY IMAGES AND YOUR WORDS.

         – HI LEE, LOVE IT. HOW DO WE
         DECIDE ON THEM?

– WE DON'T. WE PRESENT
THE IMAGES AND THE PHRASES
AND IT'S UP TO YOU TO DECIDE.

         – BASICALLY YOU GET TO MAKE
         YOUR OWN BOOK. LESS WORK FOR US.

– EXACTLY. JUST NEED A TITLE.
ANY IDEAS?

         – TO BE HONEST I COULDN'T
         CARE LESS.

– PERFECT"

THOMAS LÉLU & LEE SHULMAN
AN ANONYMOUS PROJECT

COULDN'T CARE
LESS

JBE BOOKS

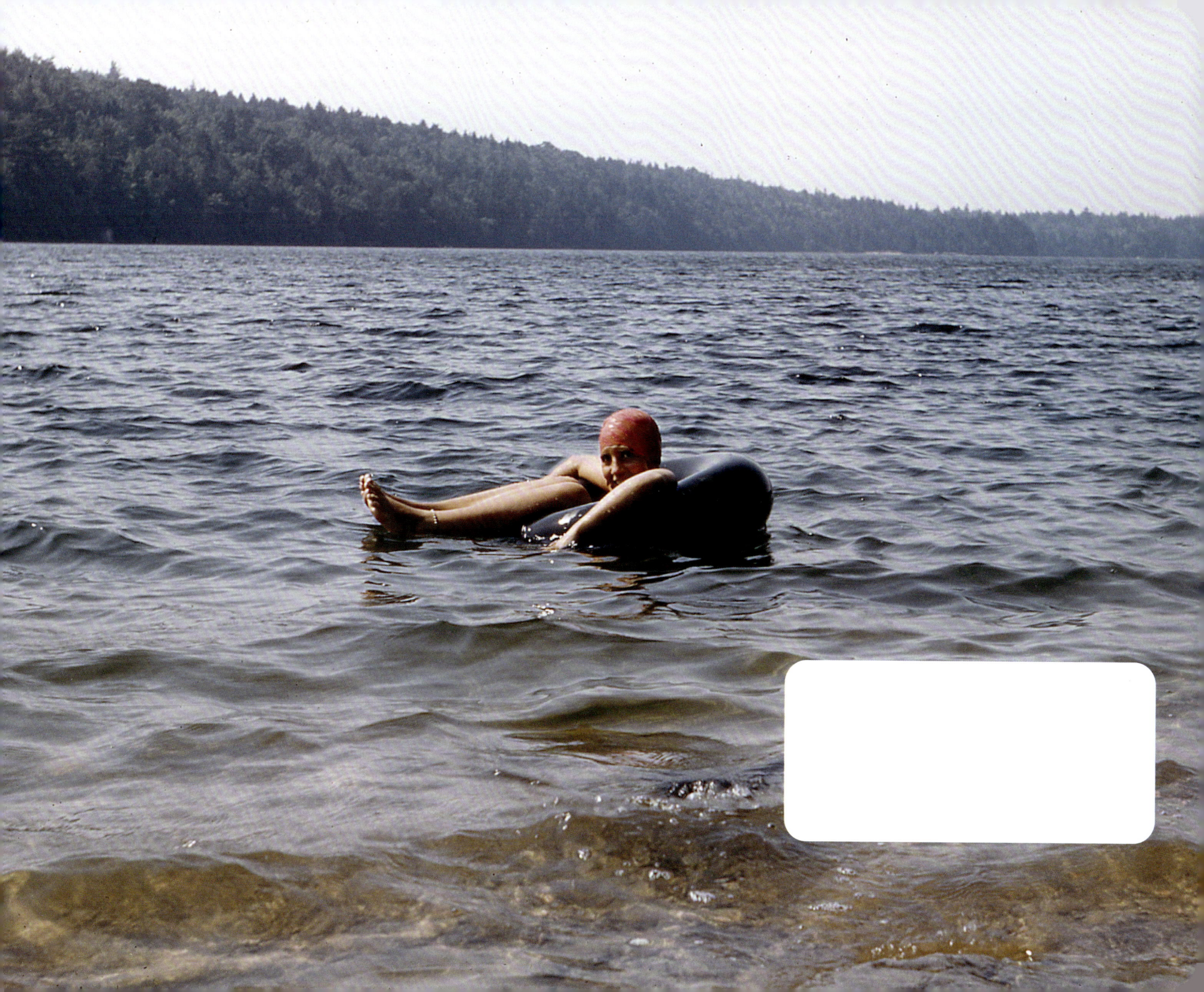

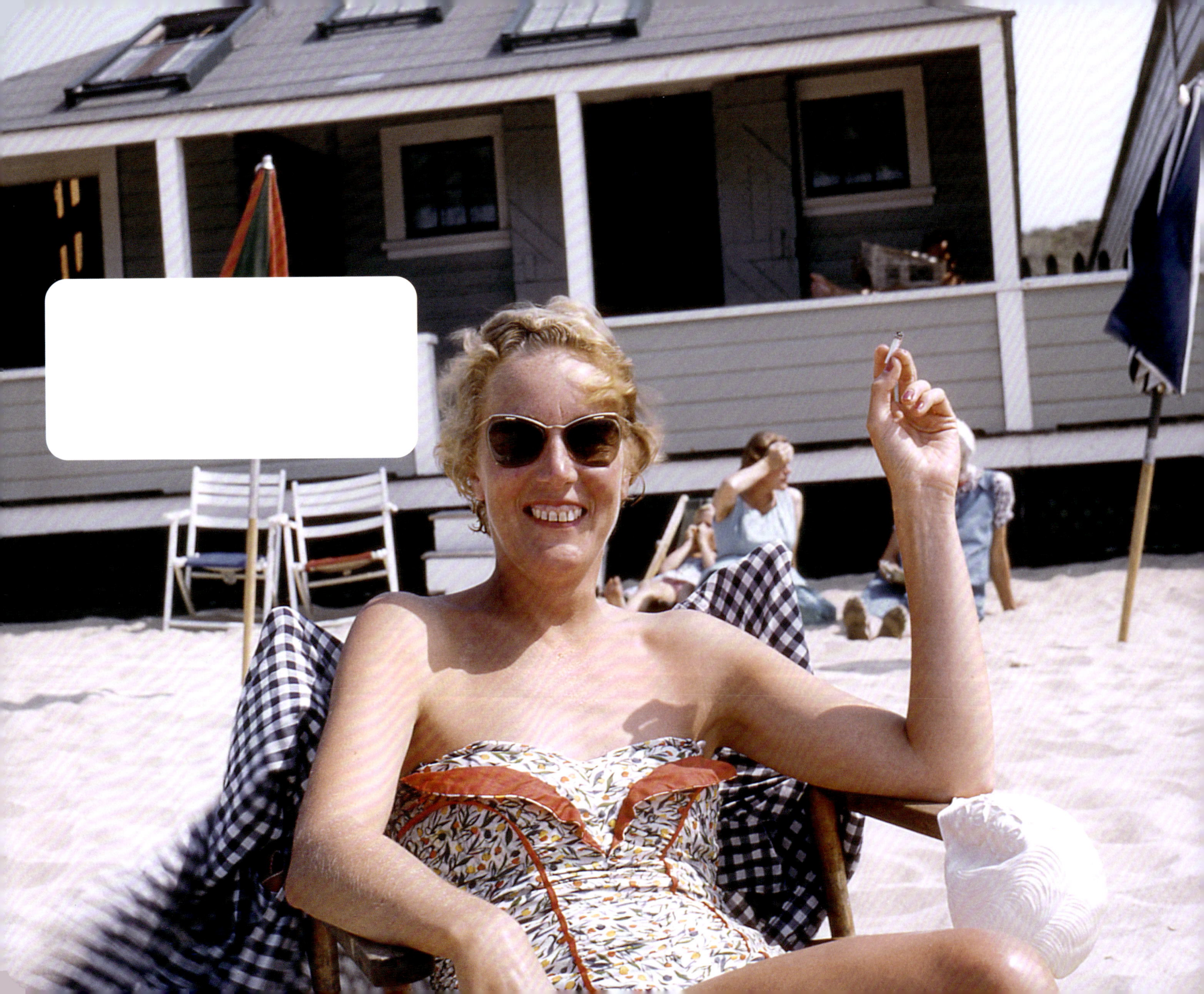

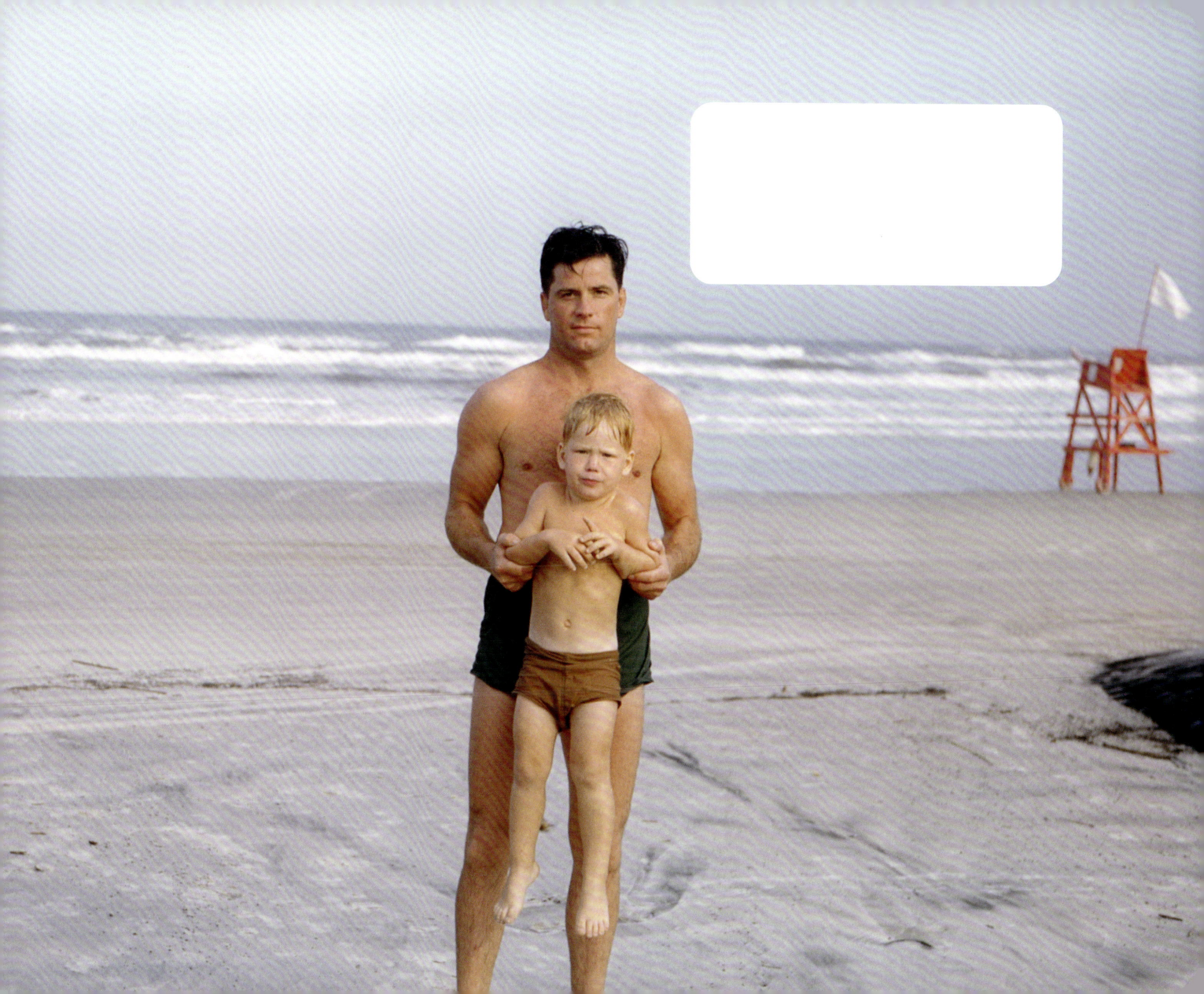

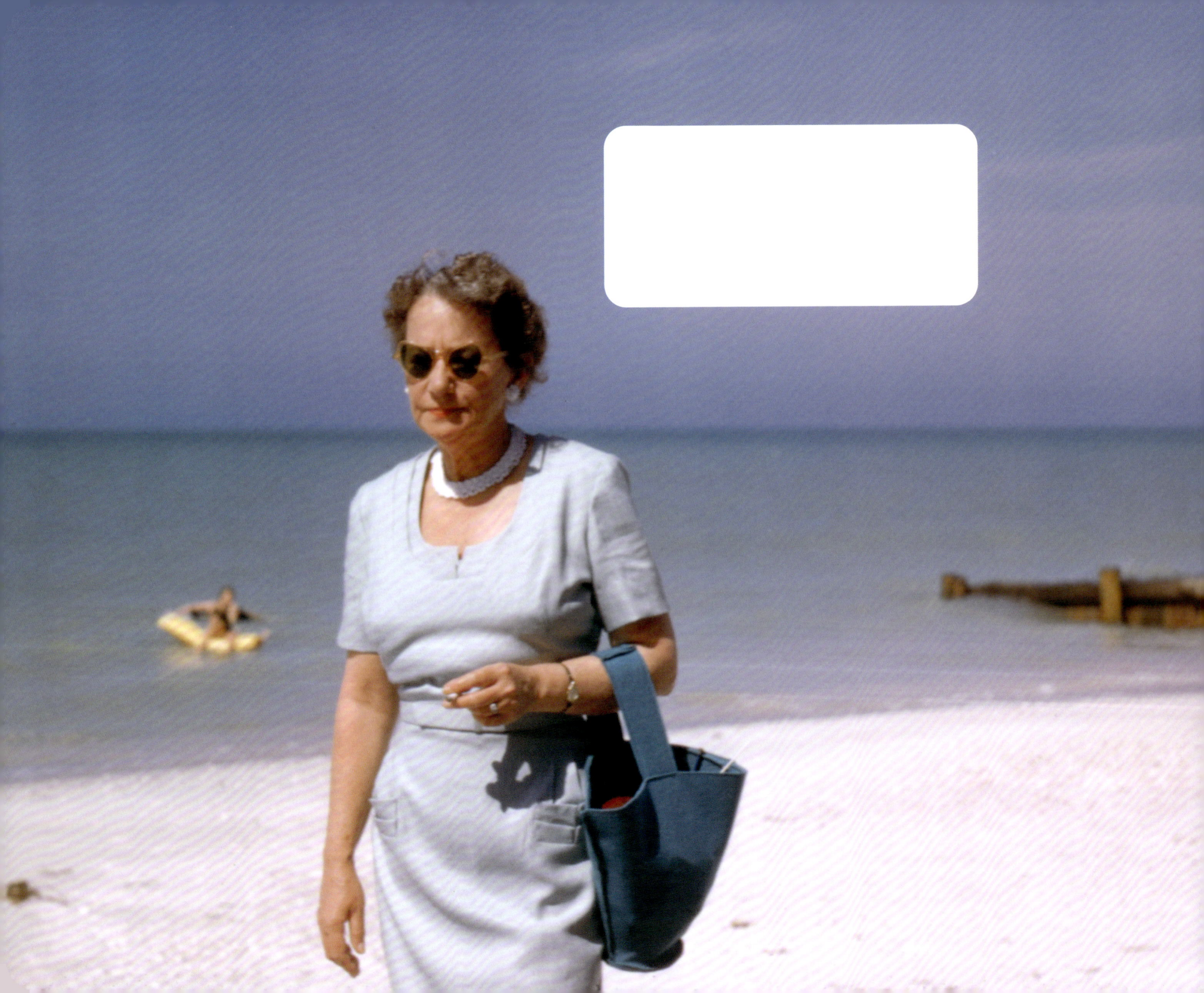

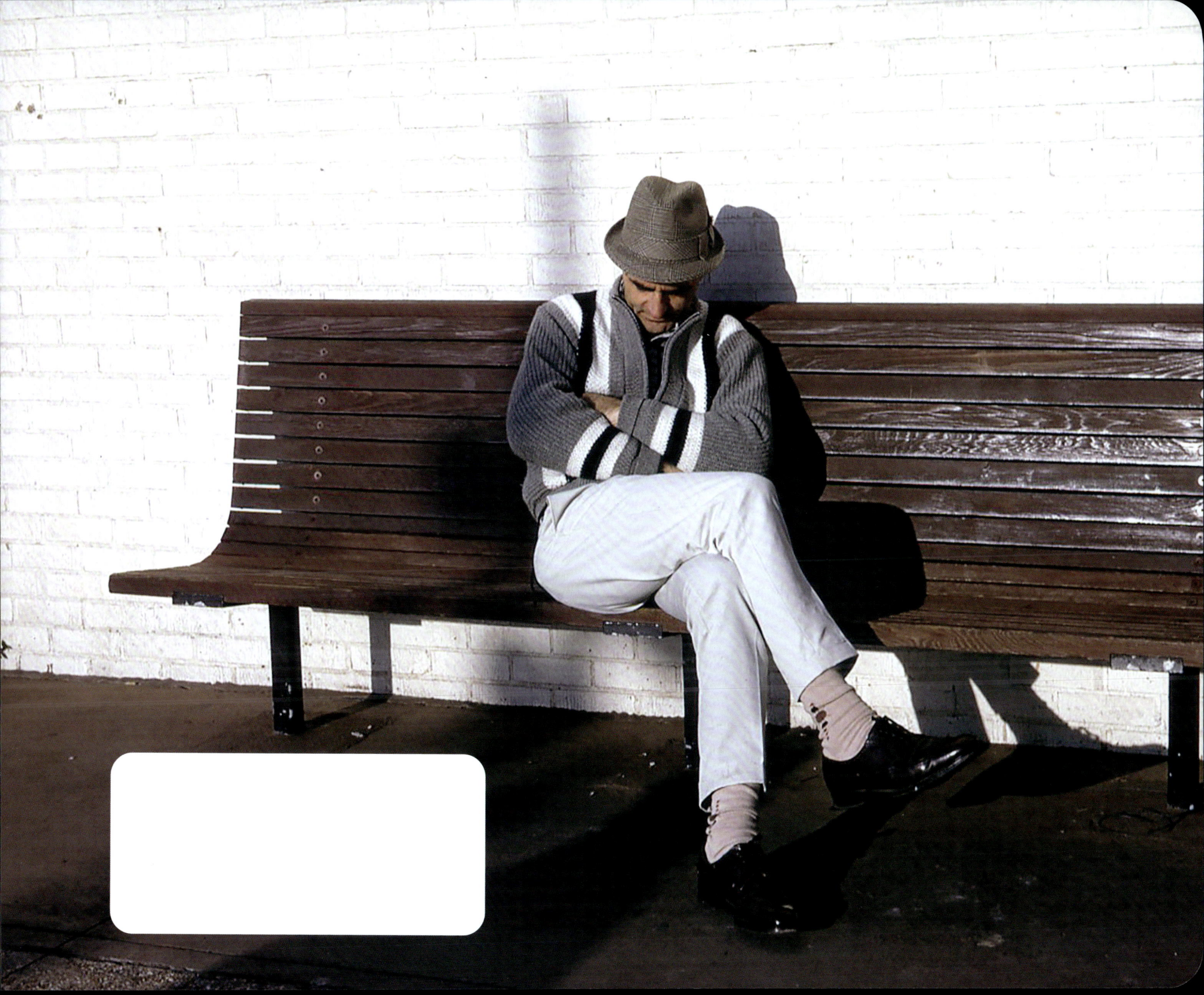

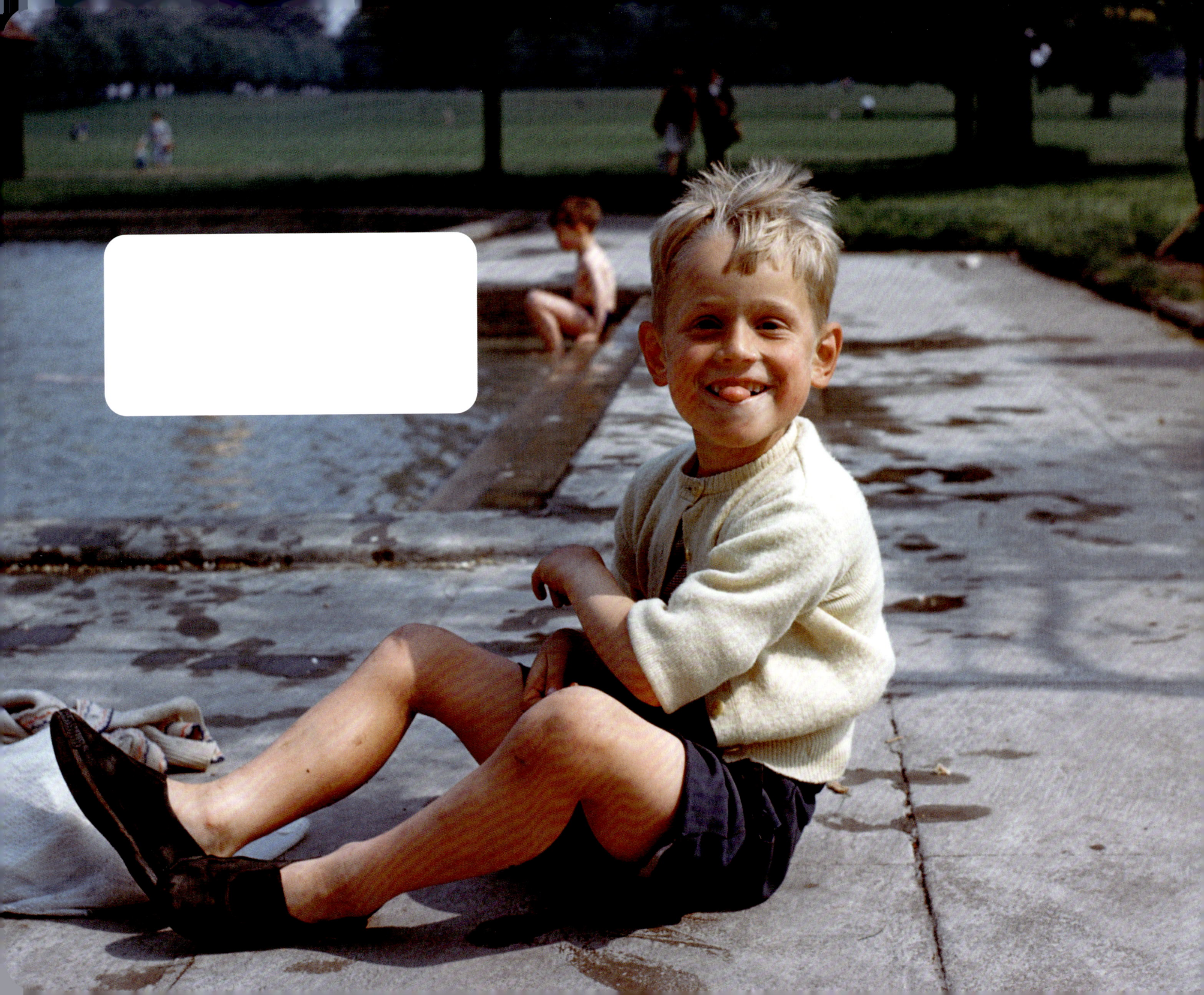

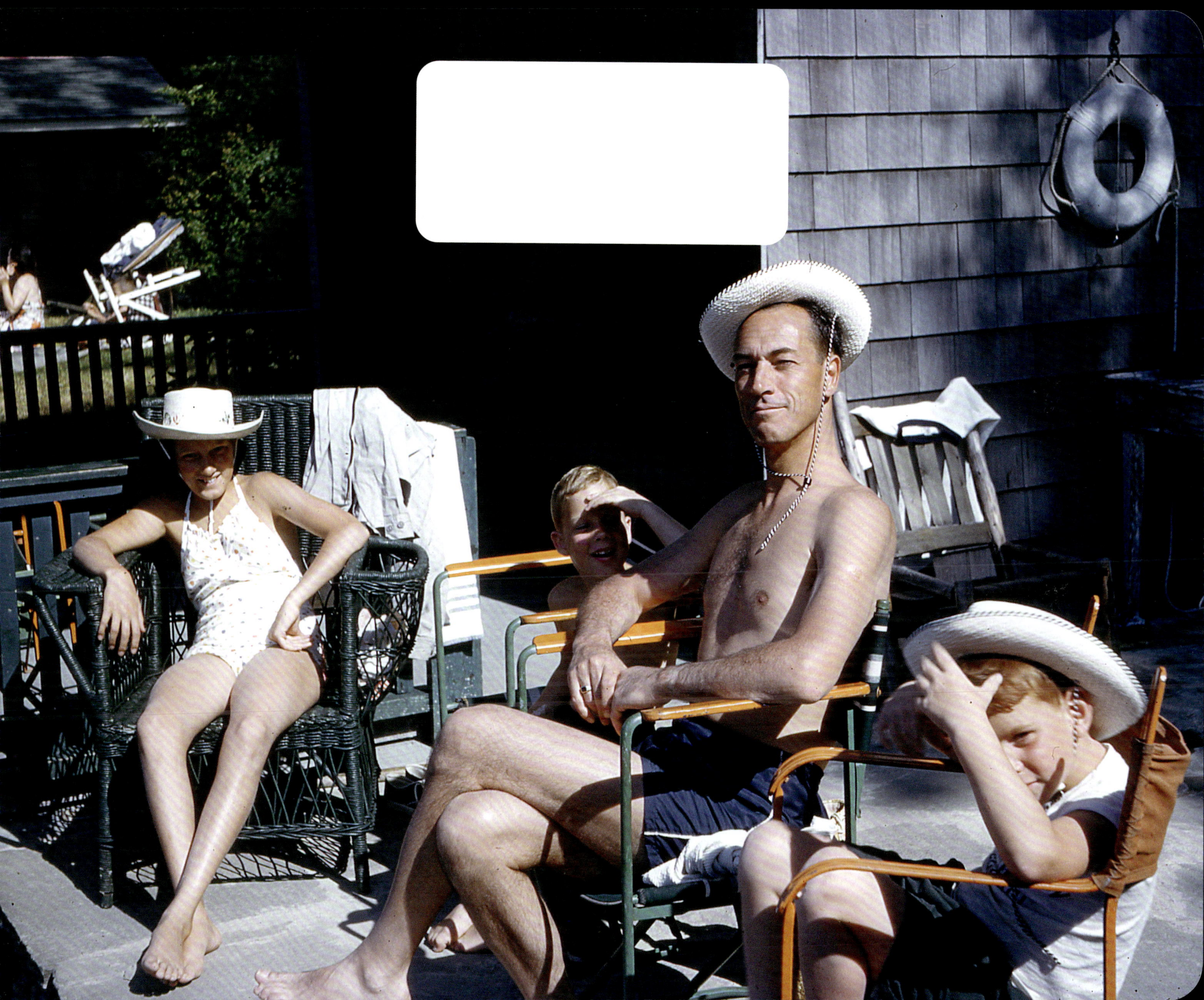

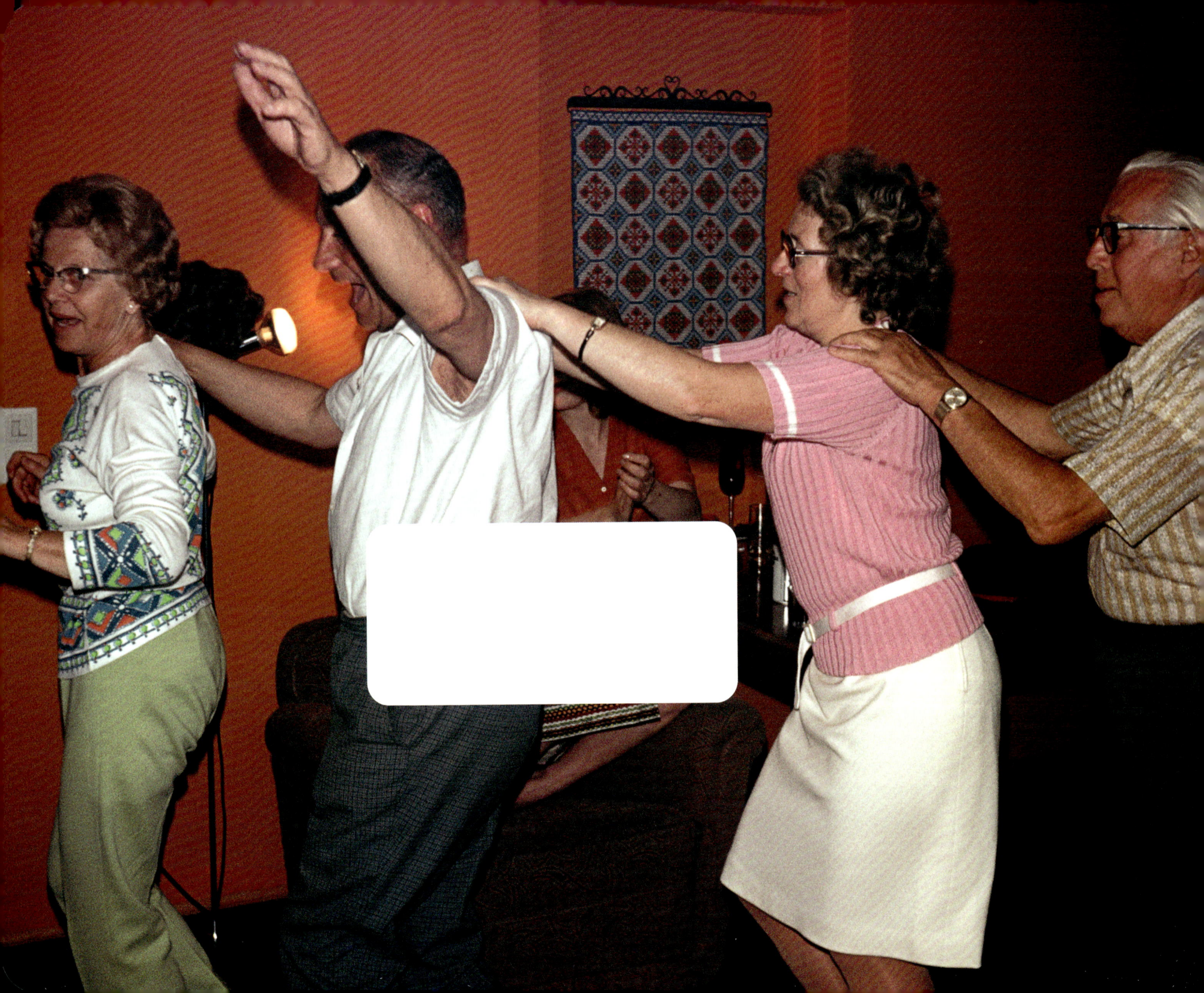

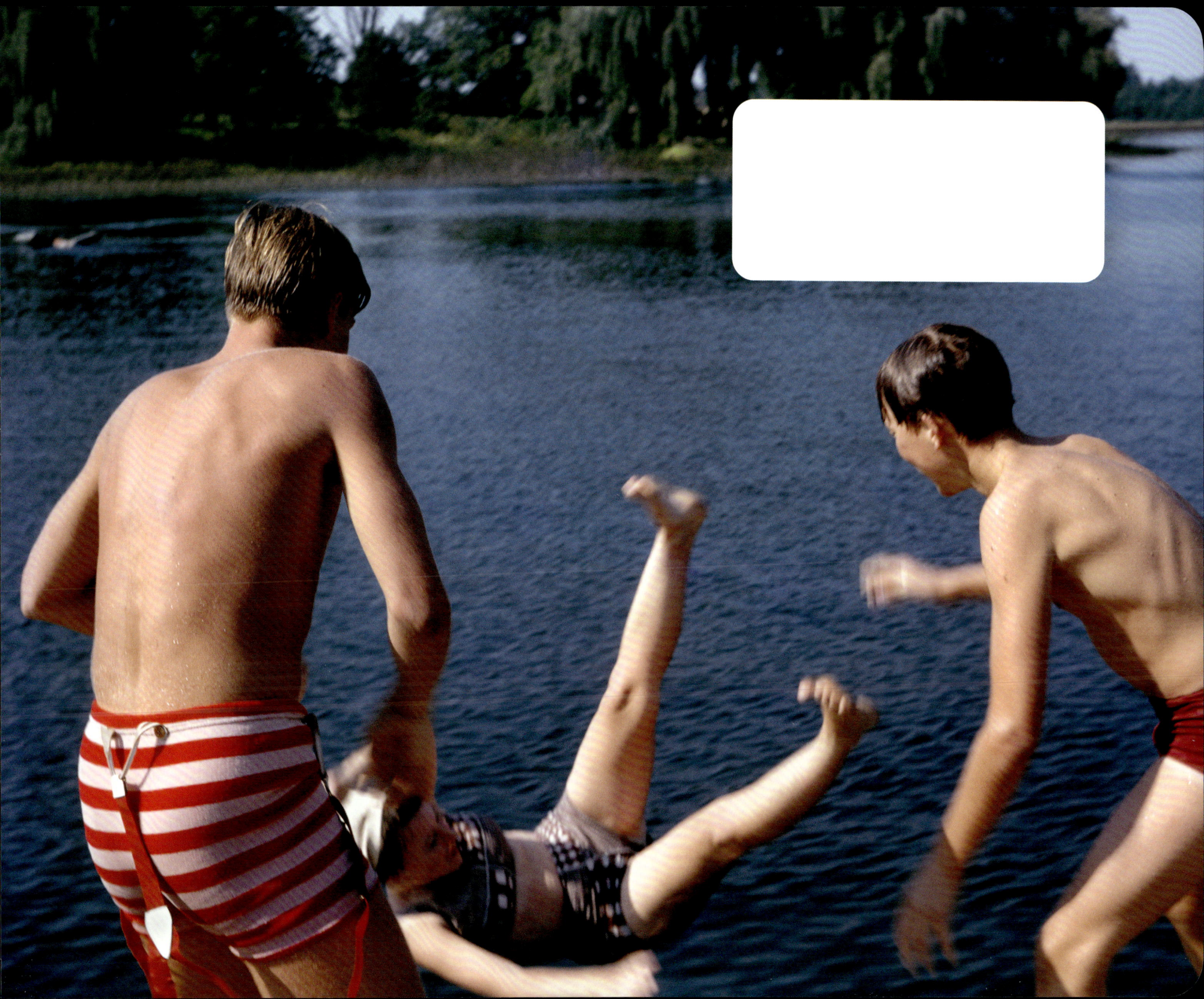

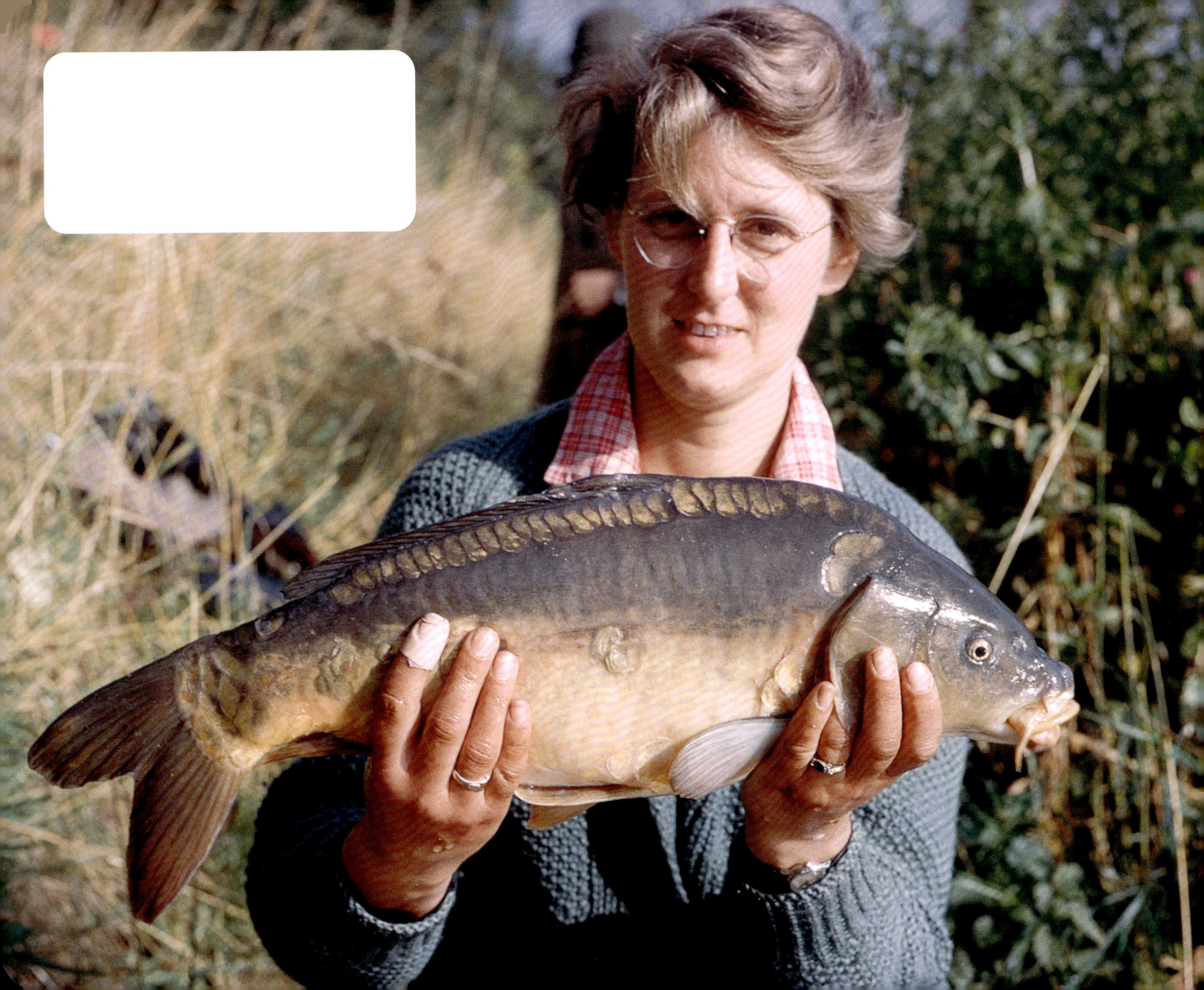

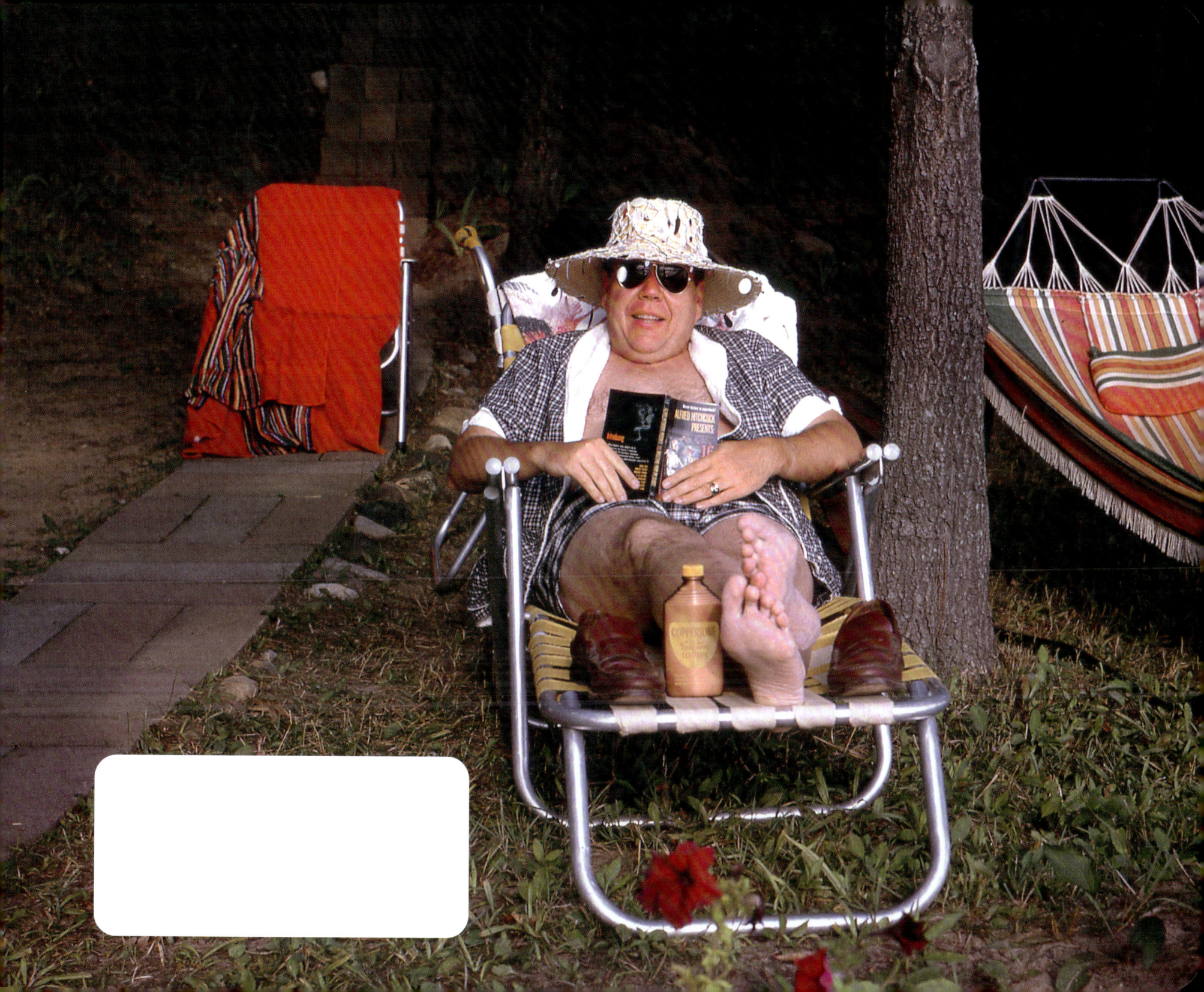

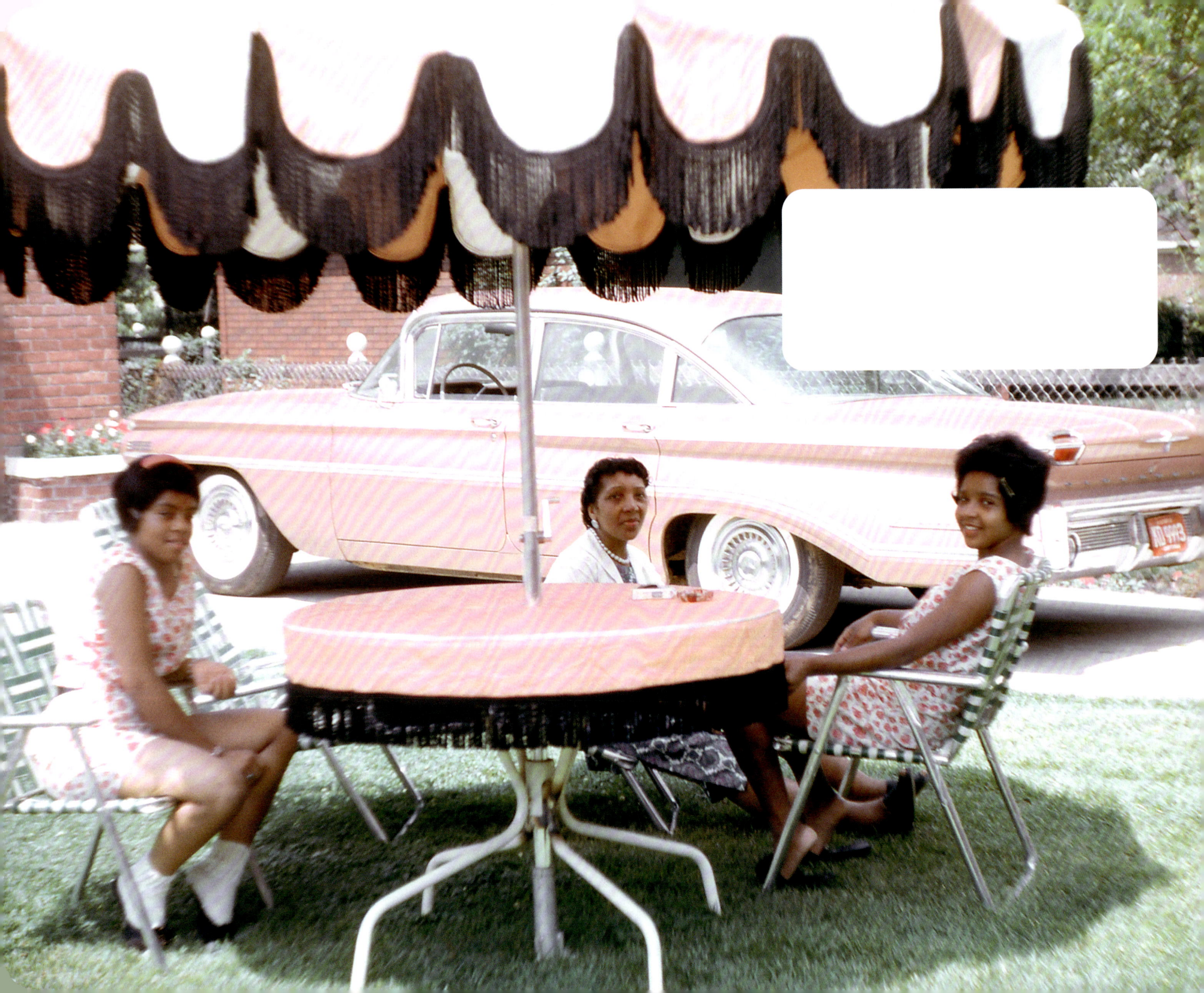

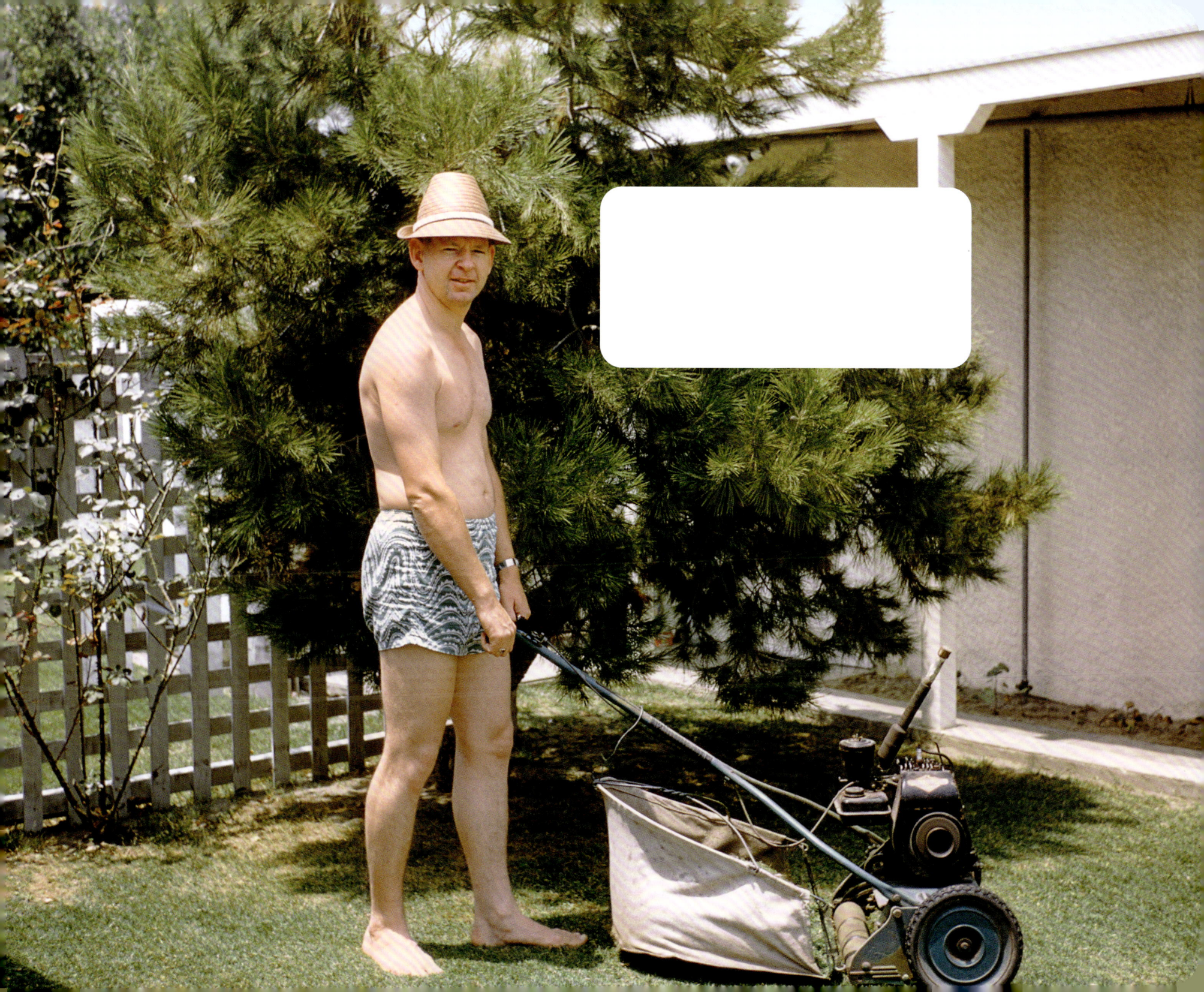

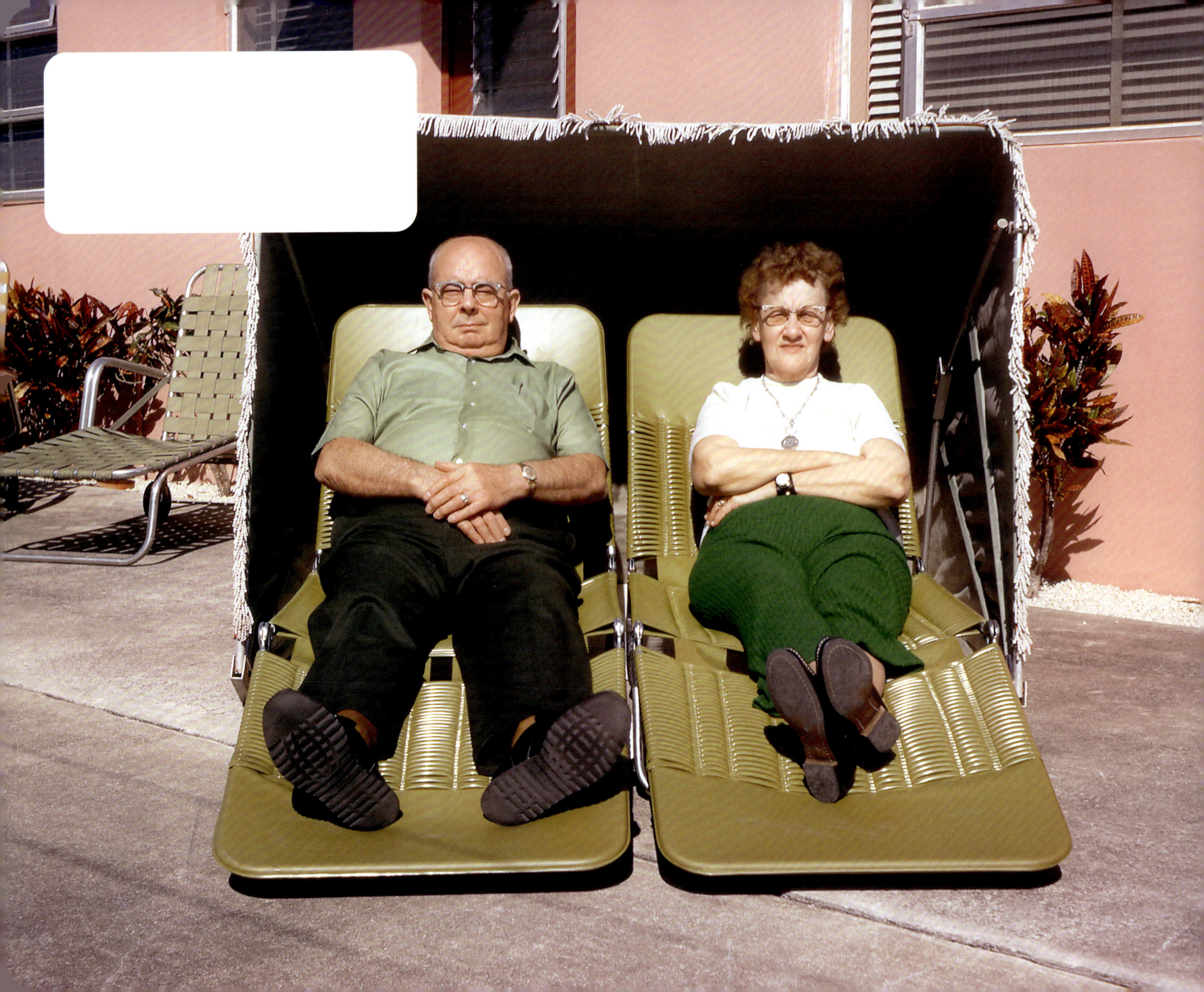

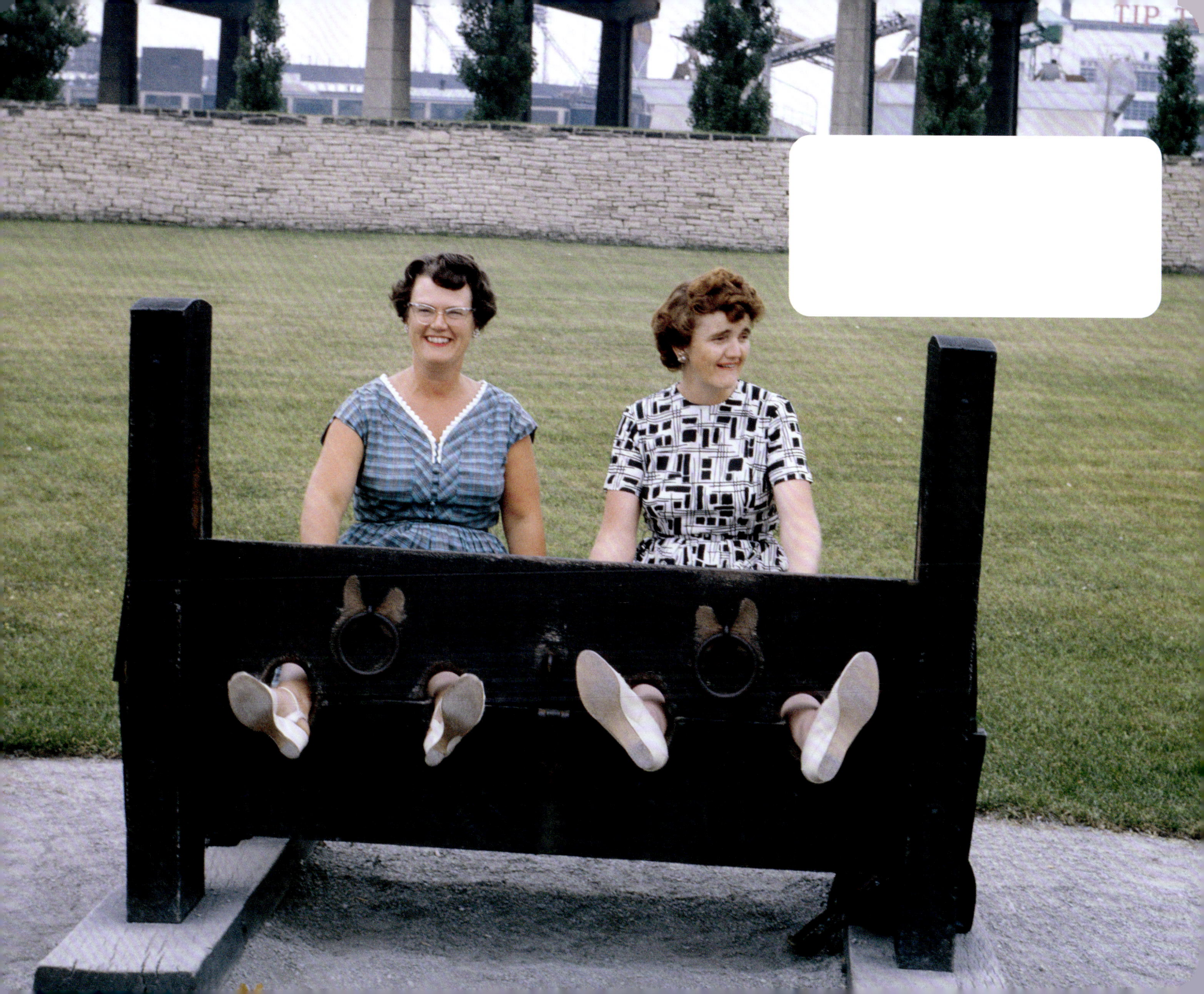

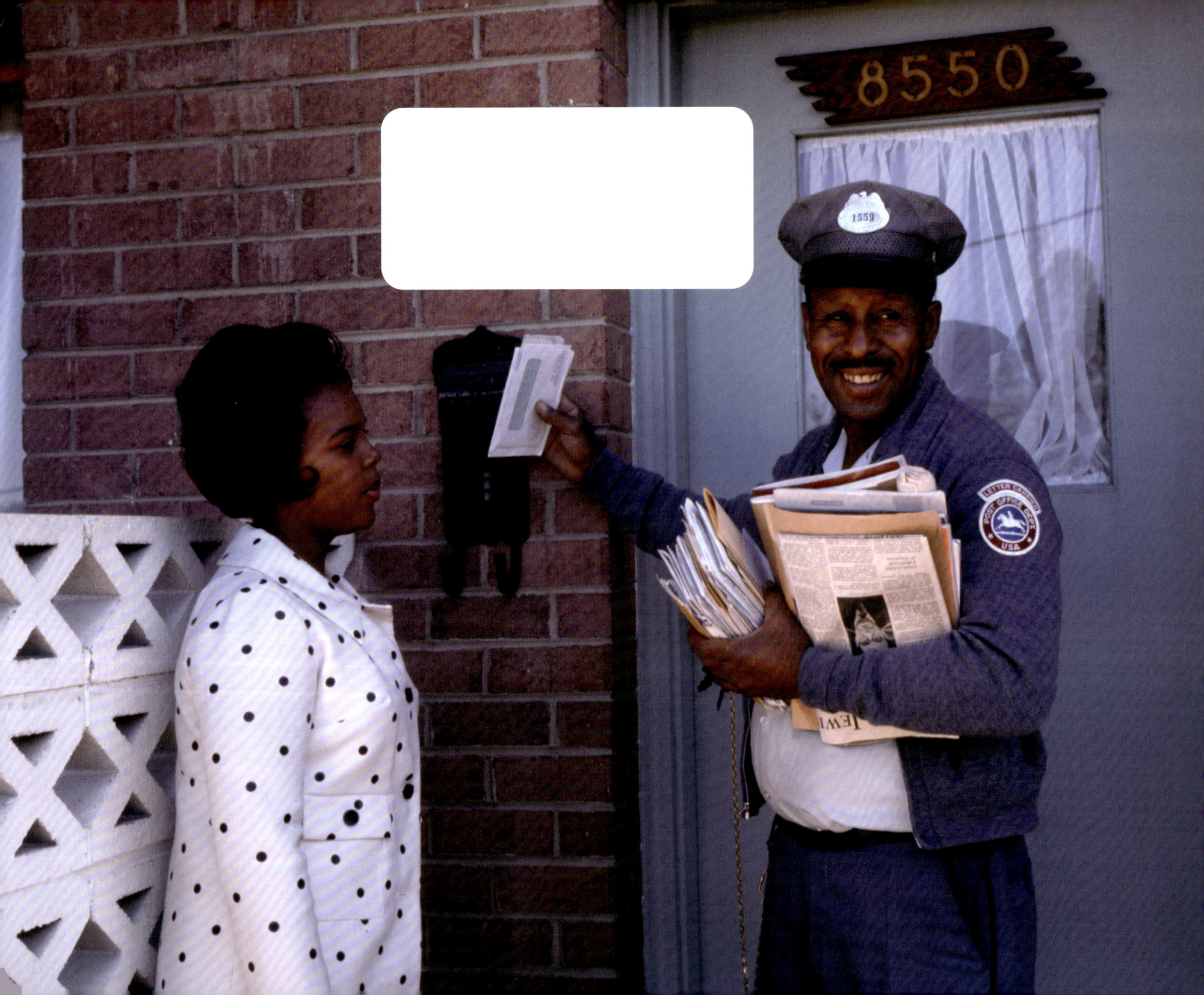

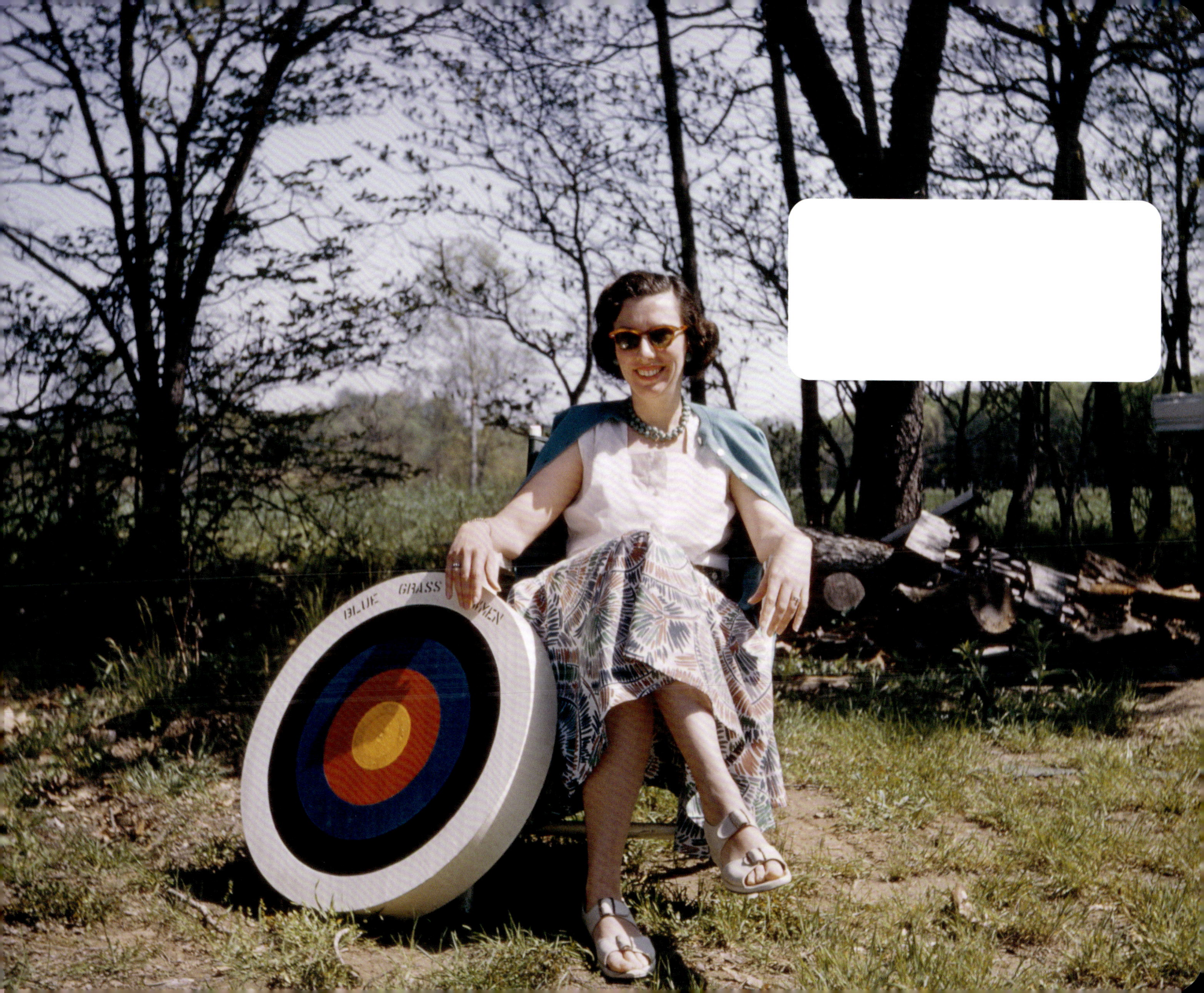

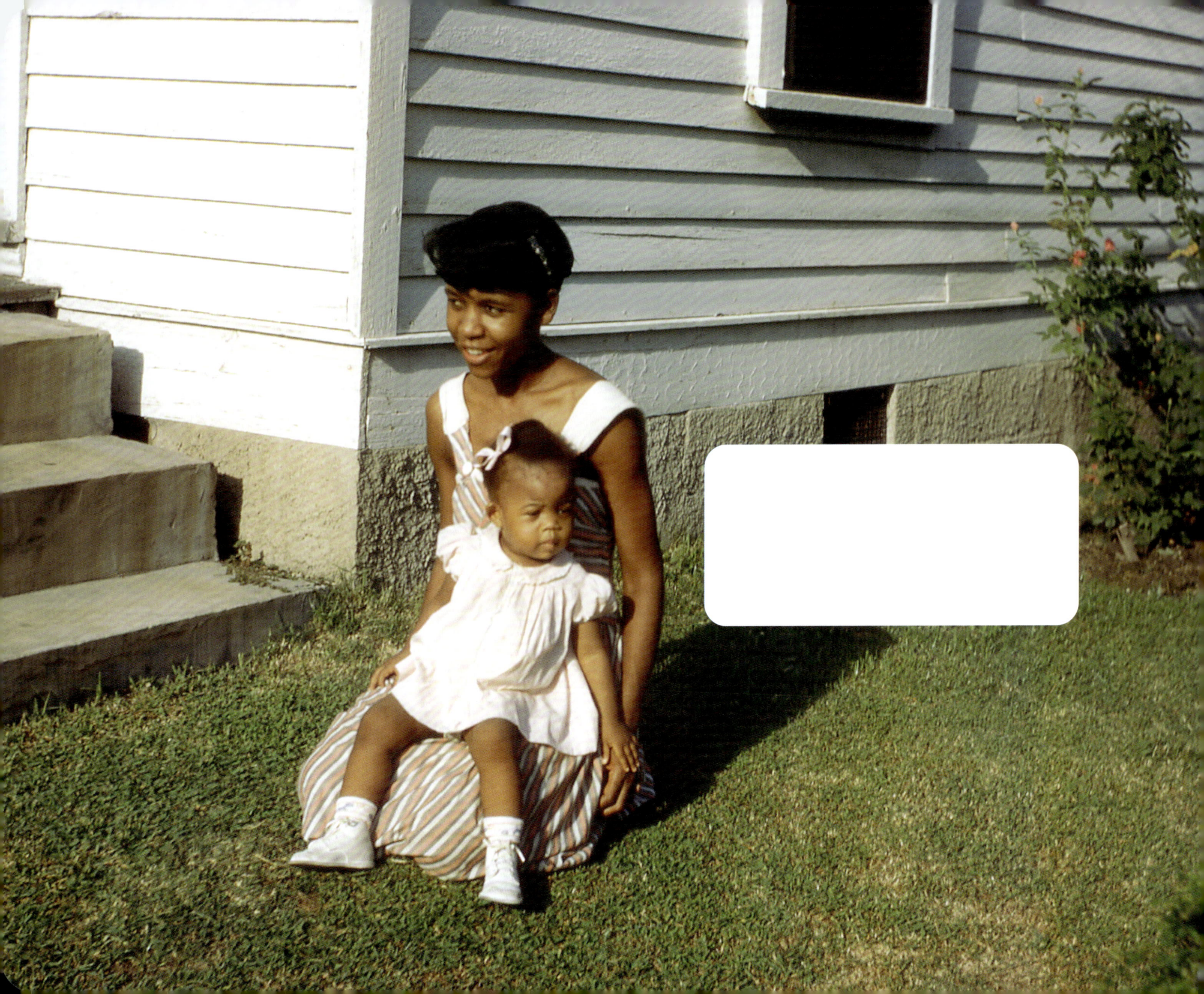

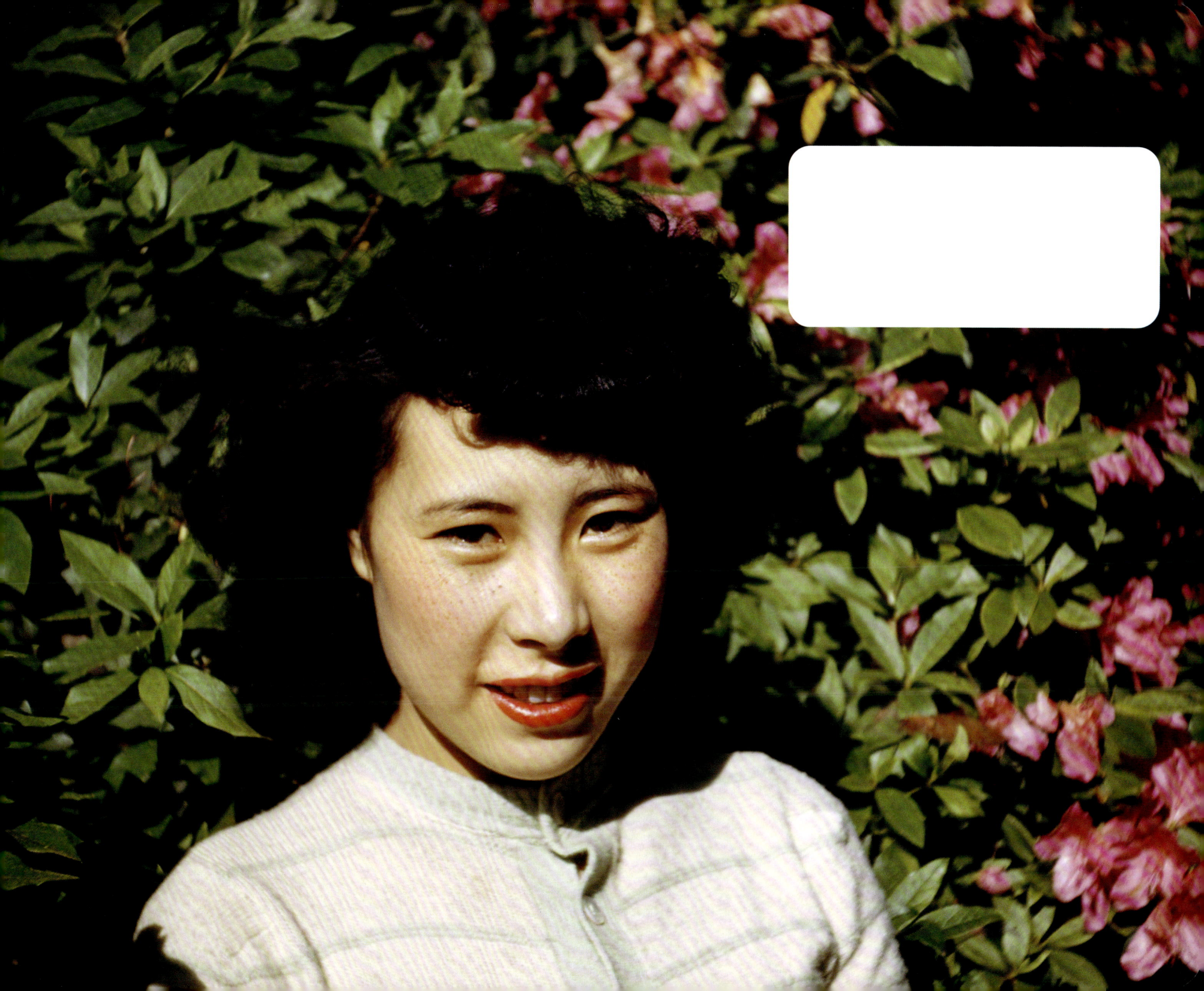

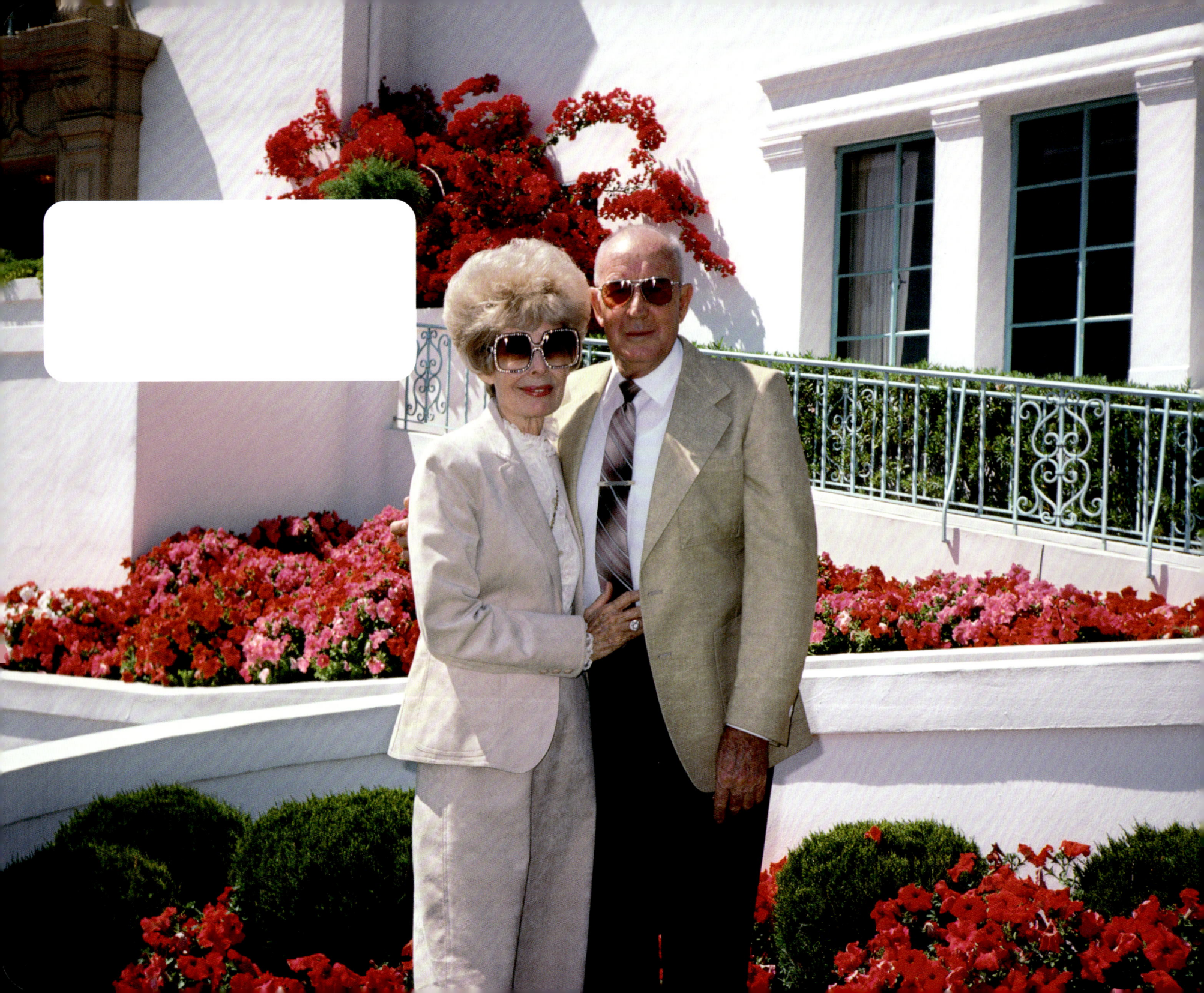

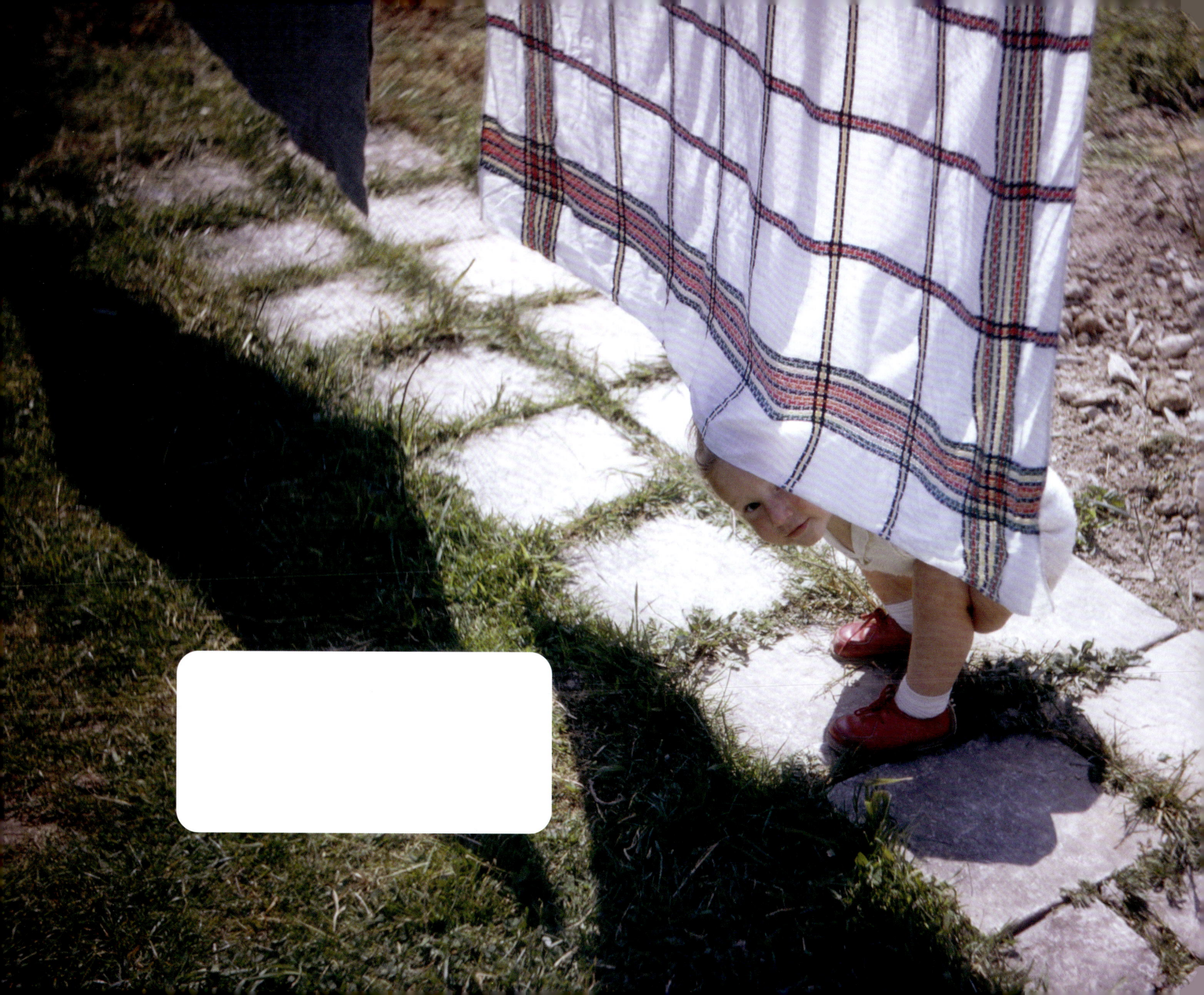

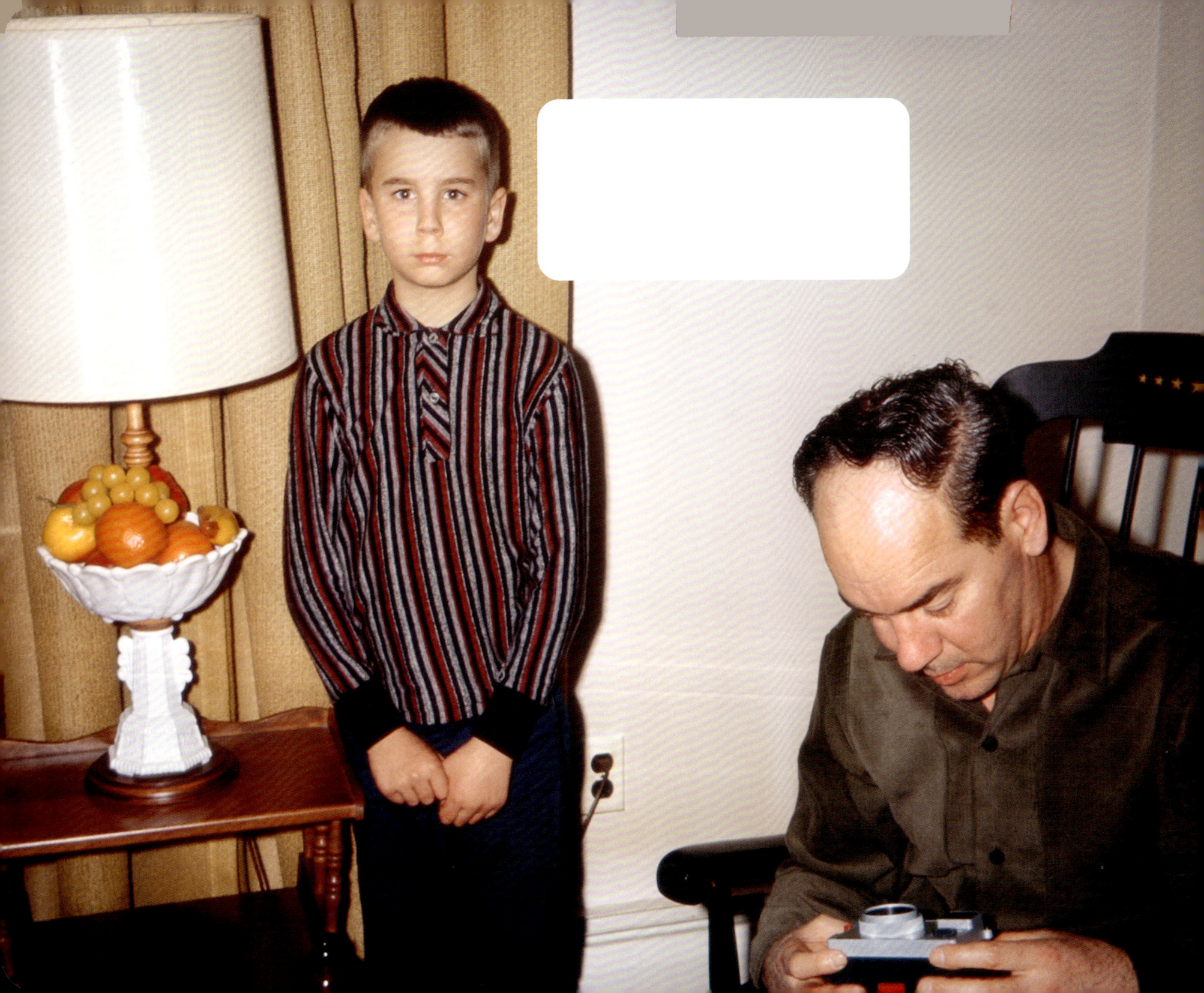

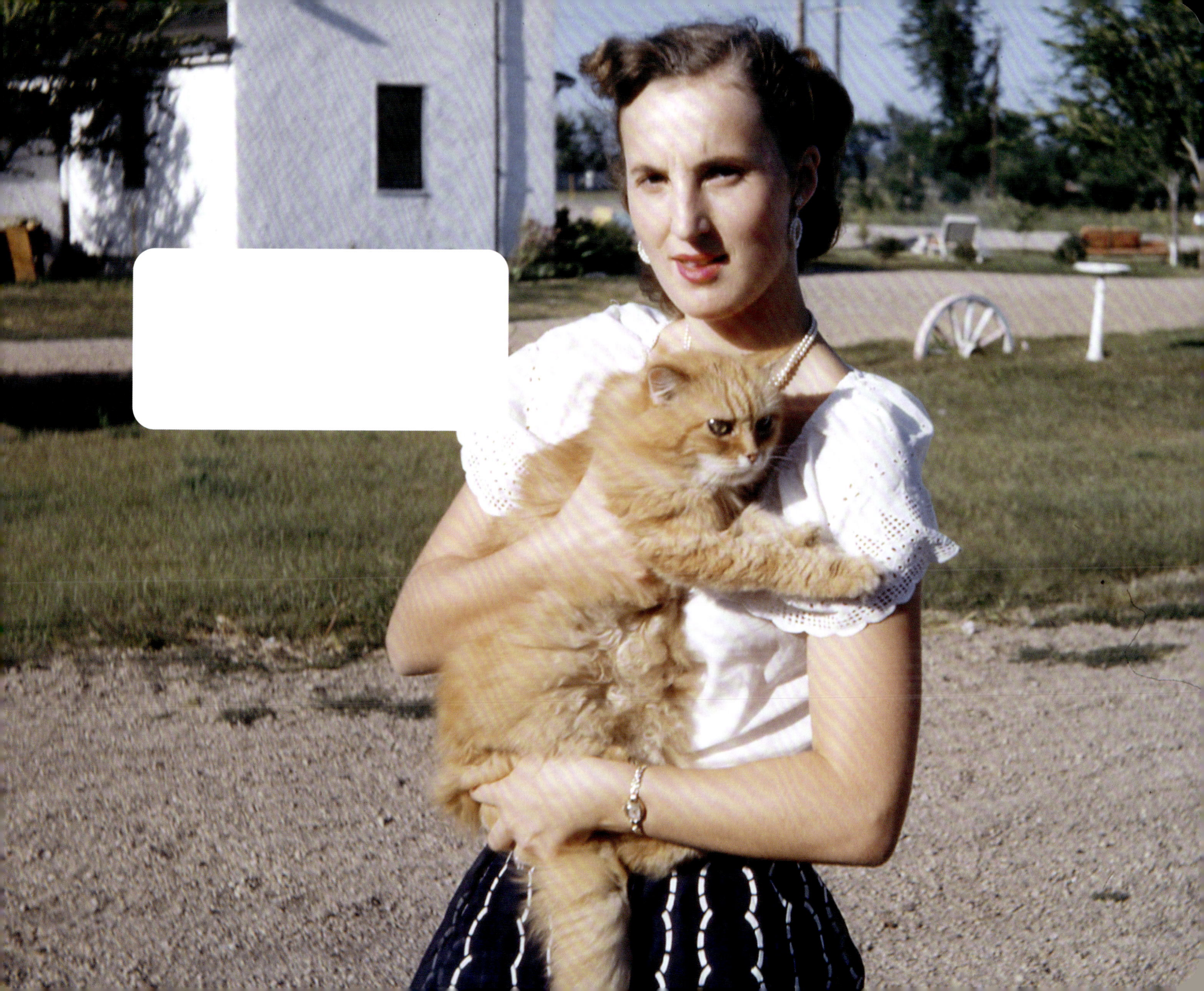

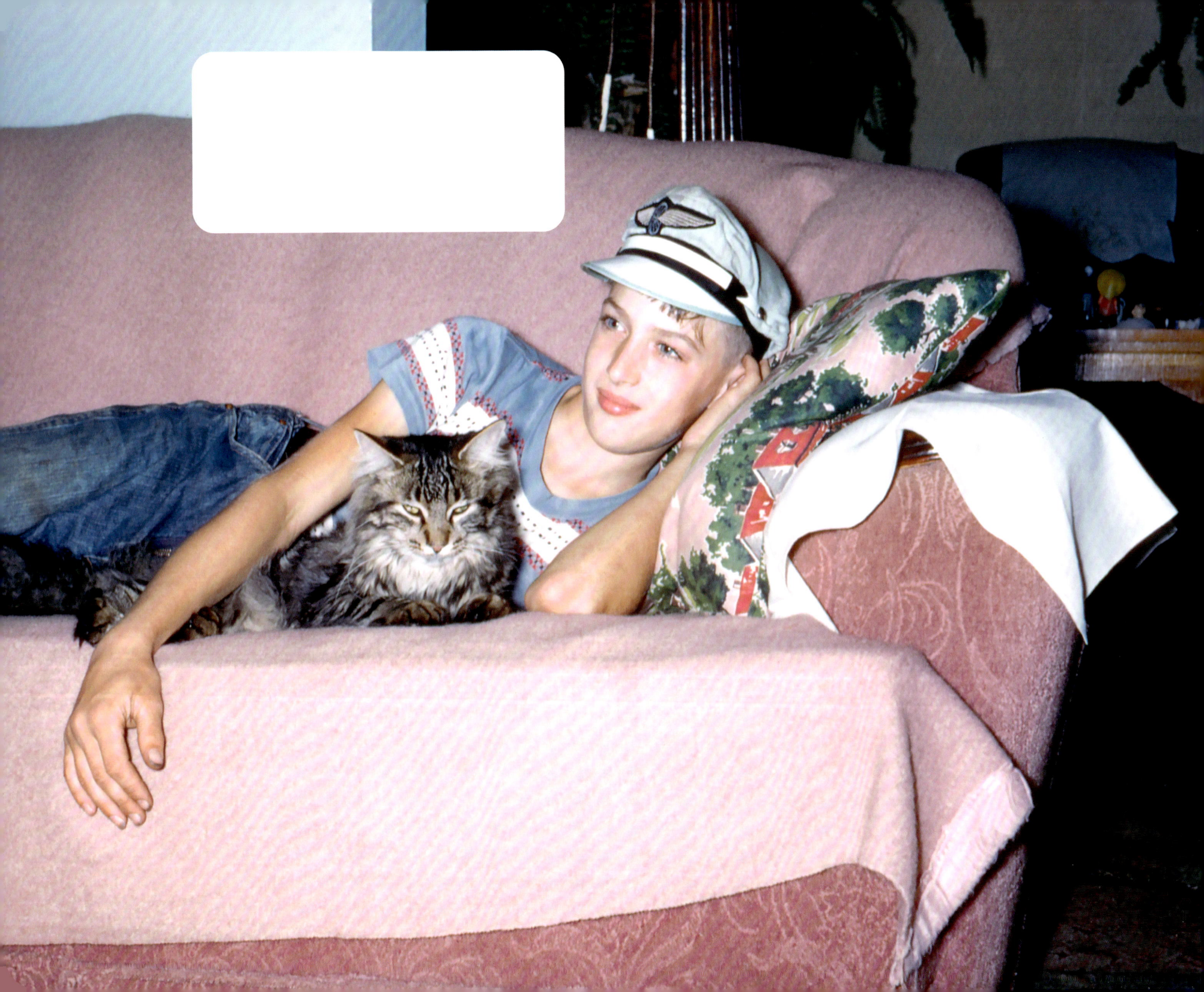

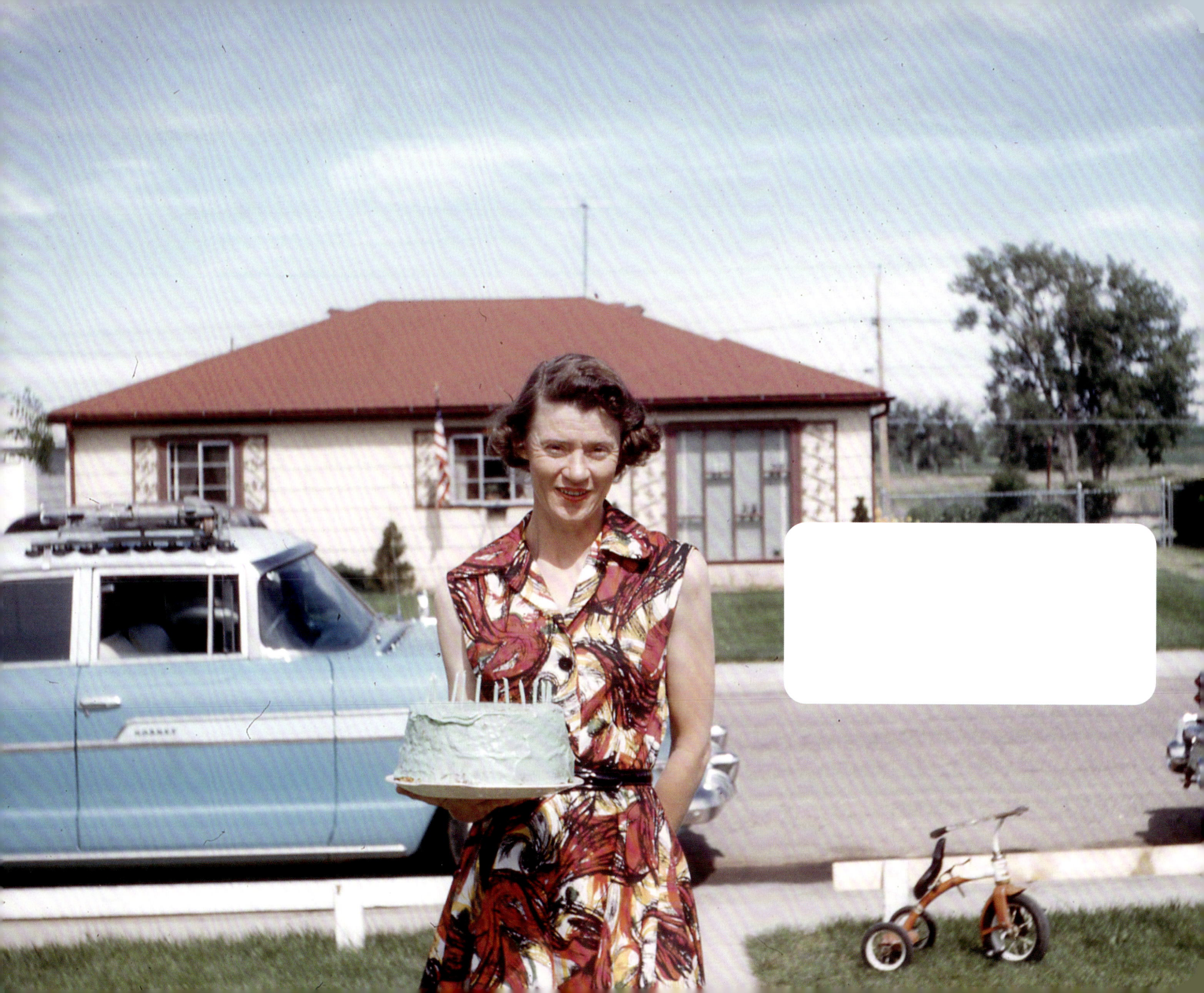

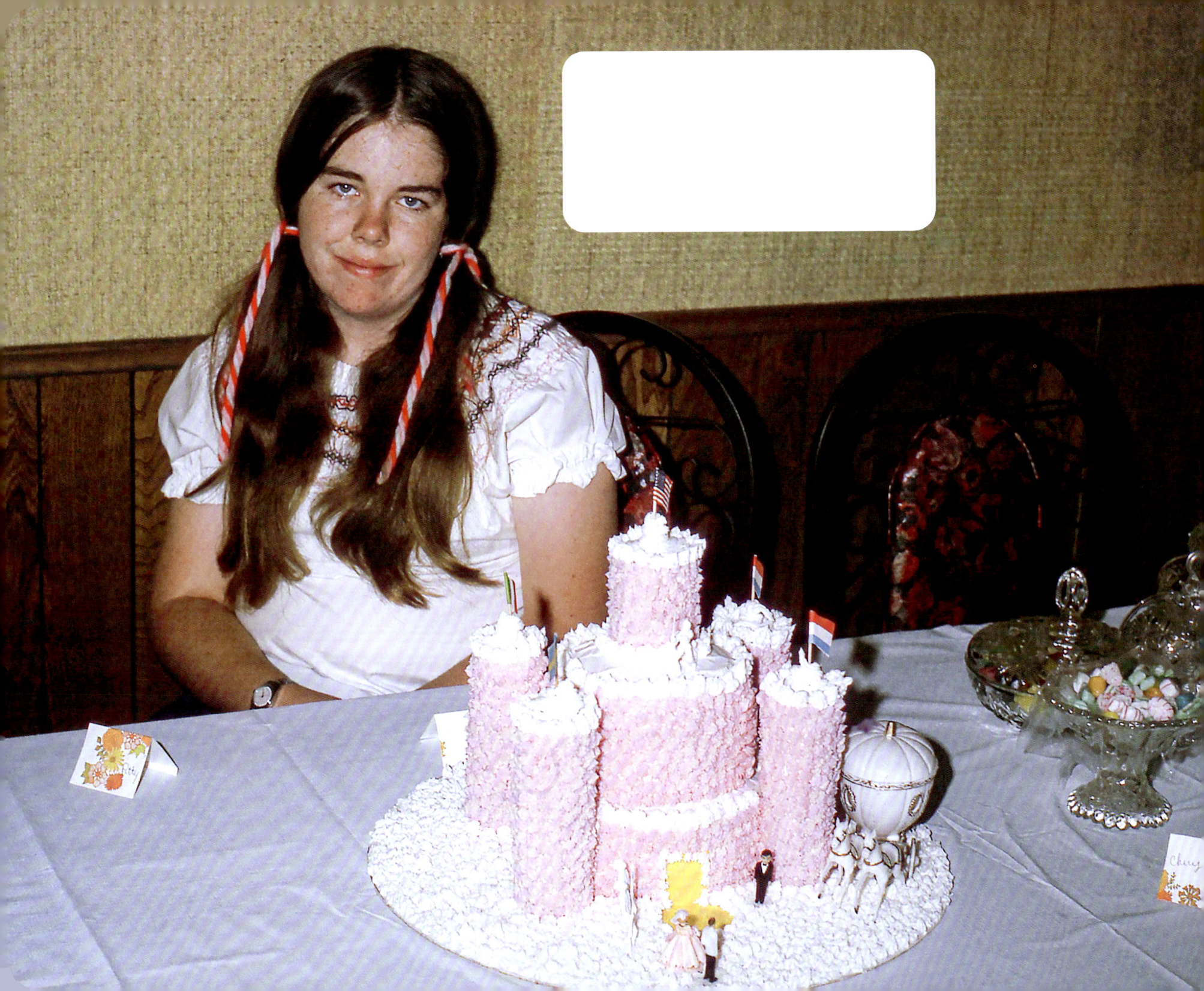

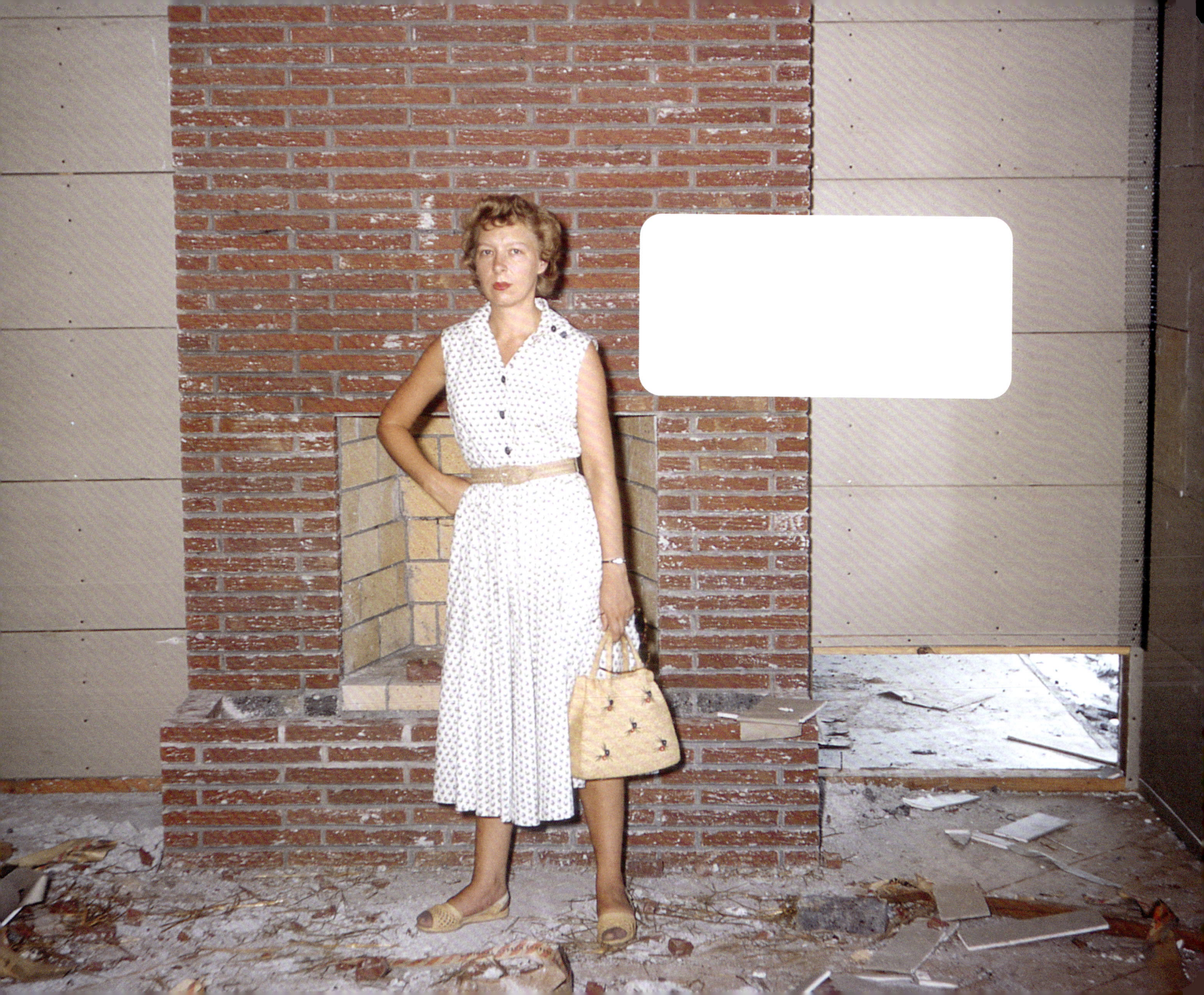

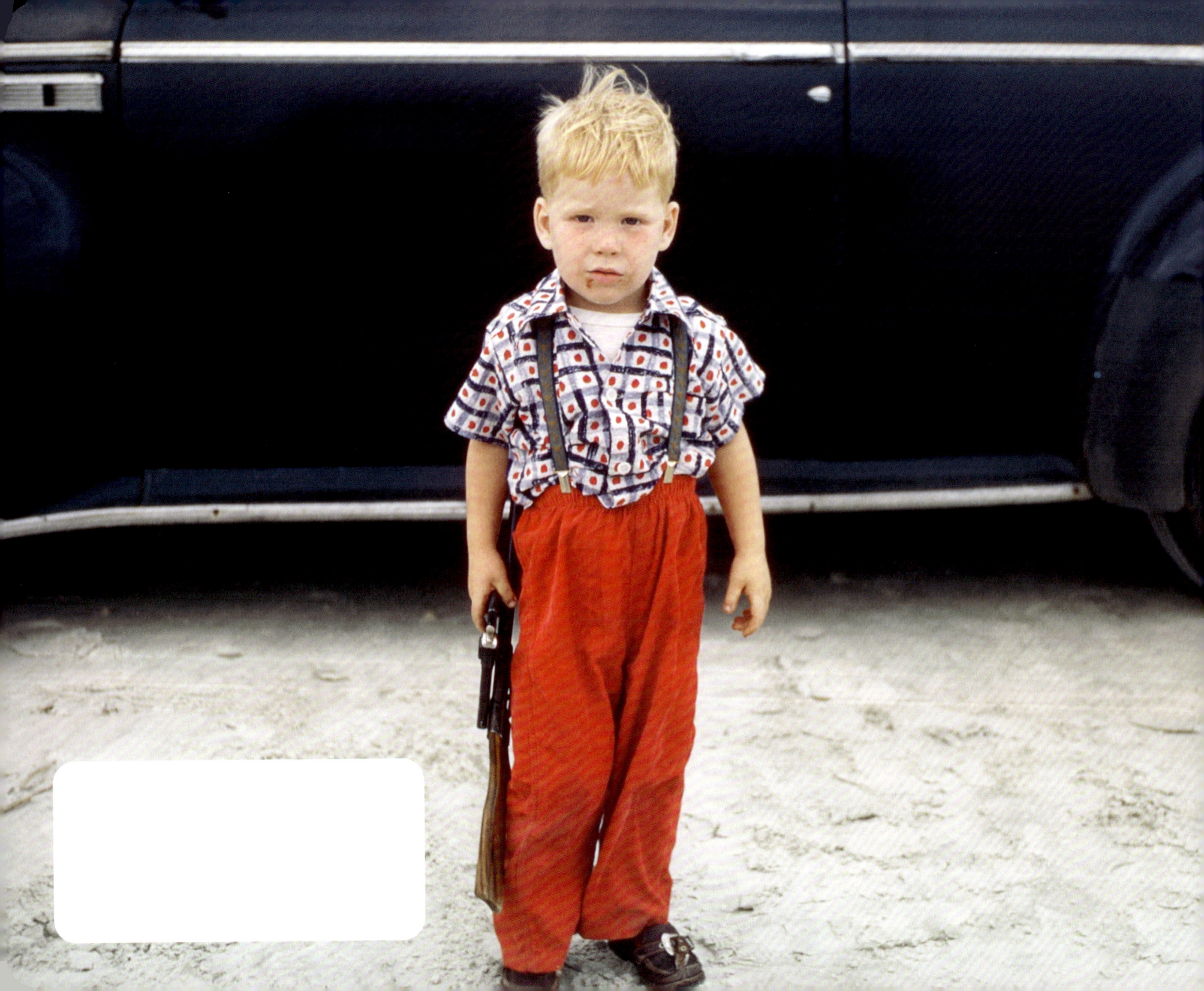

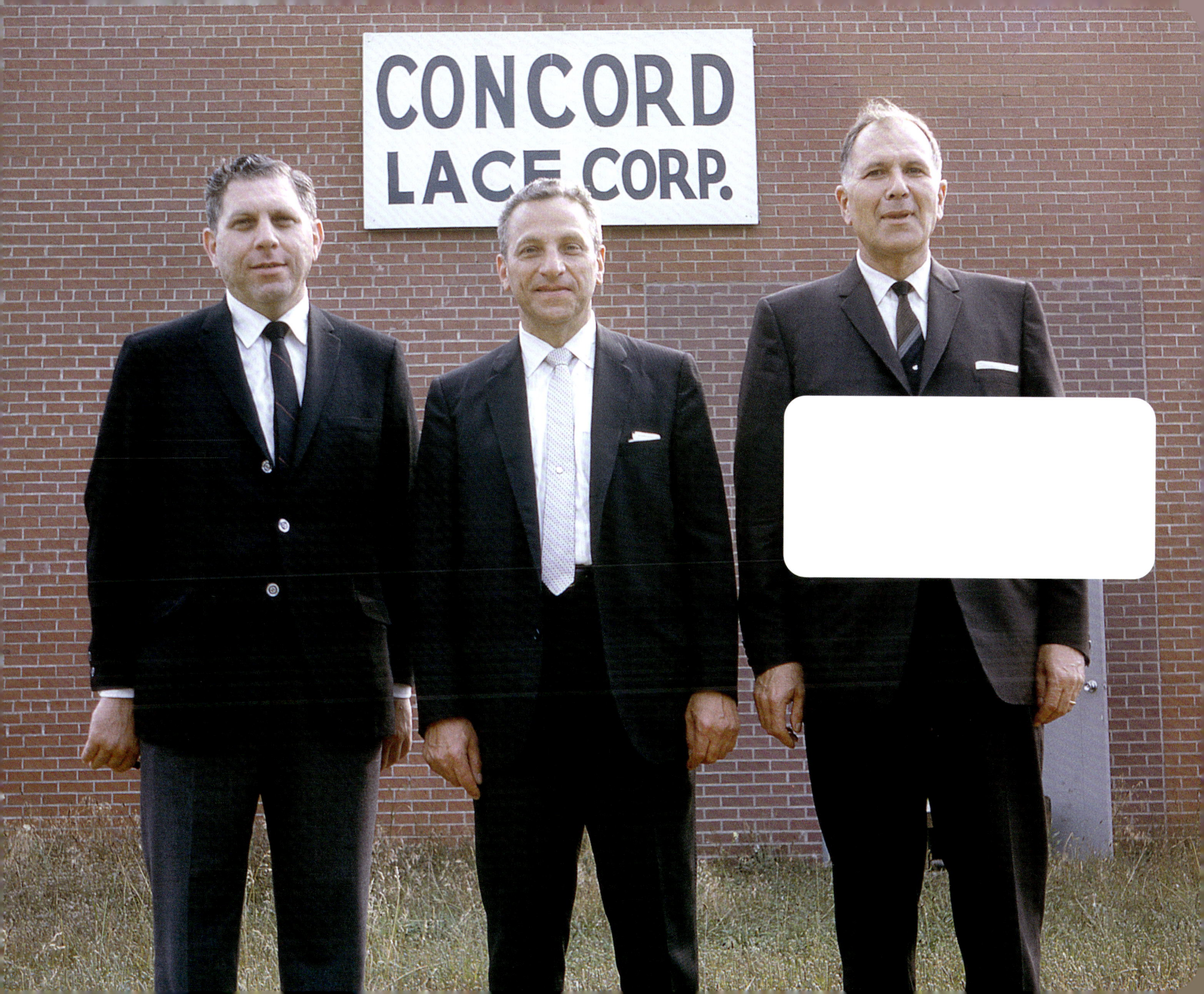

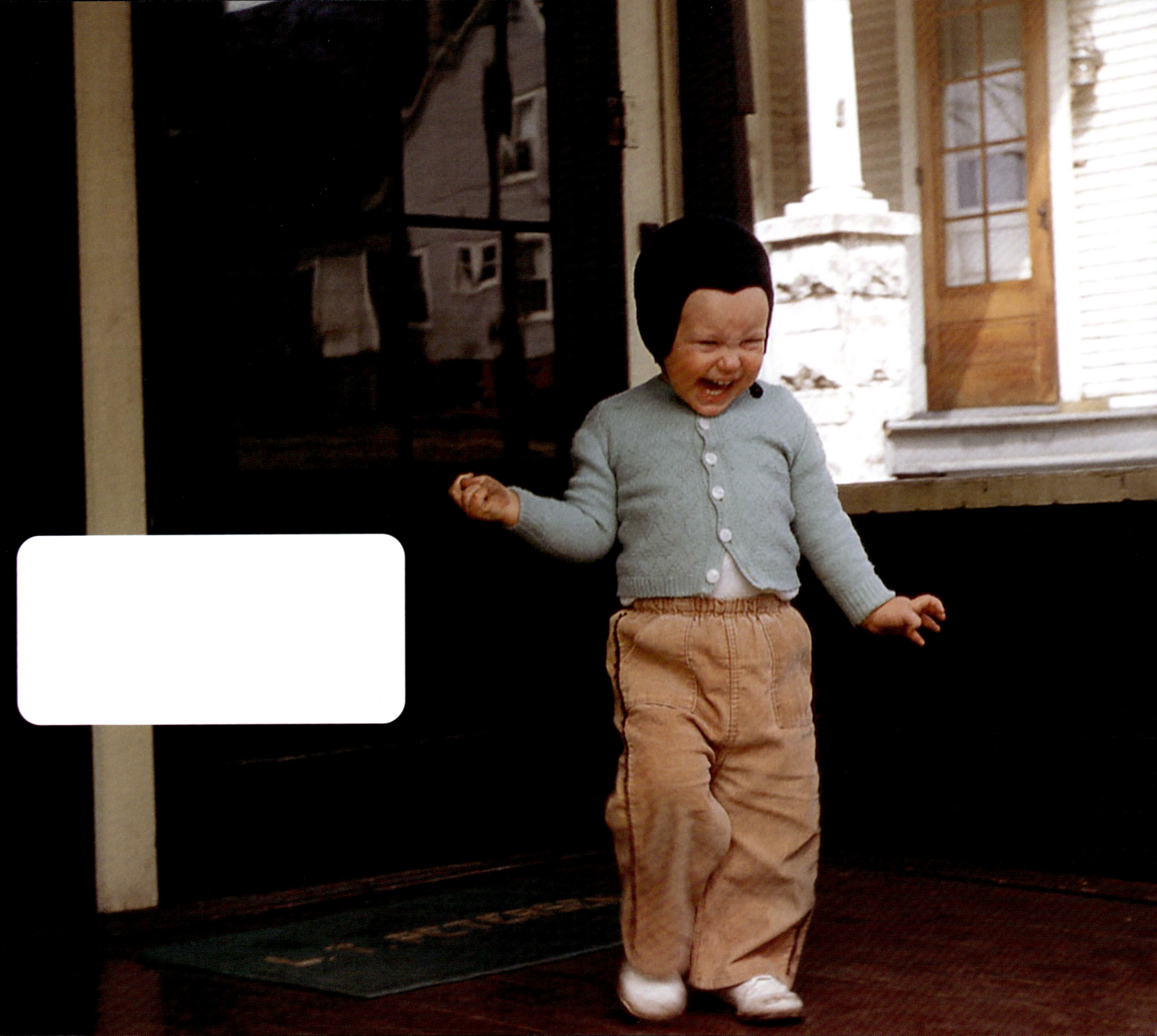

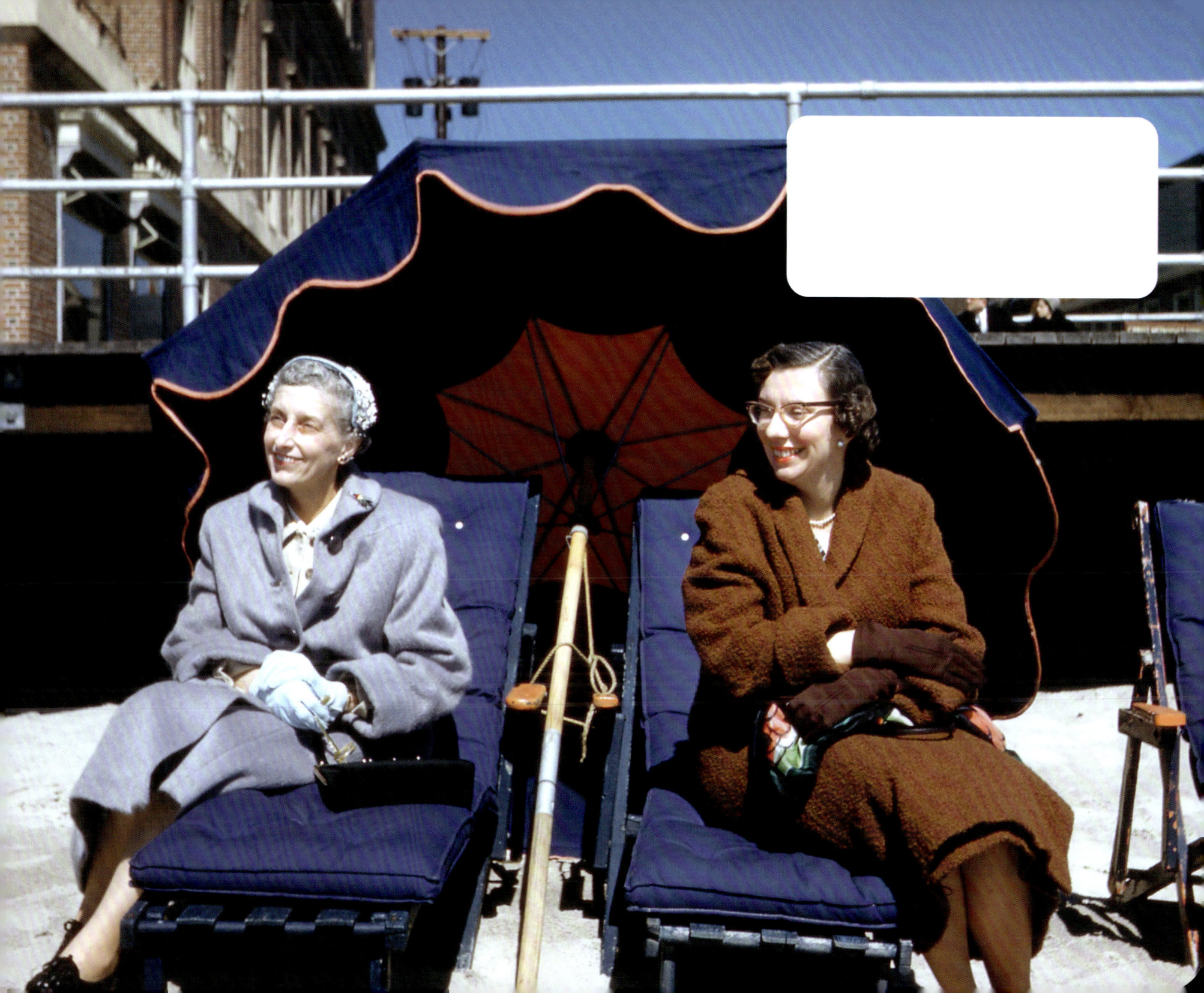

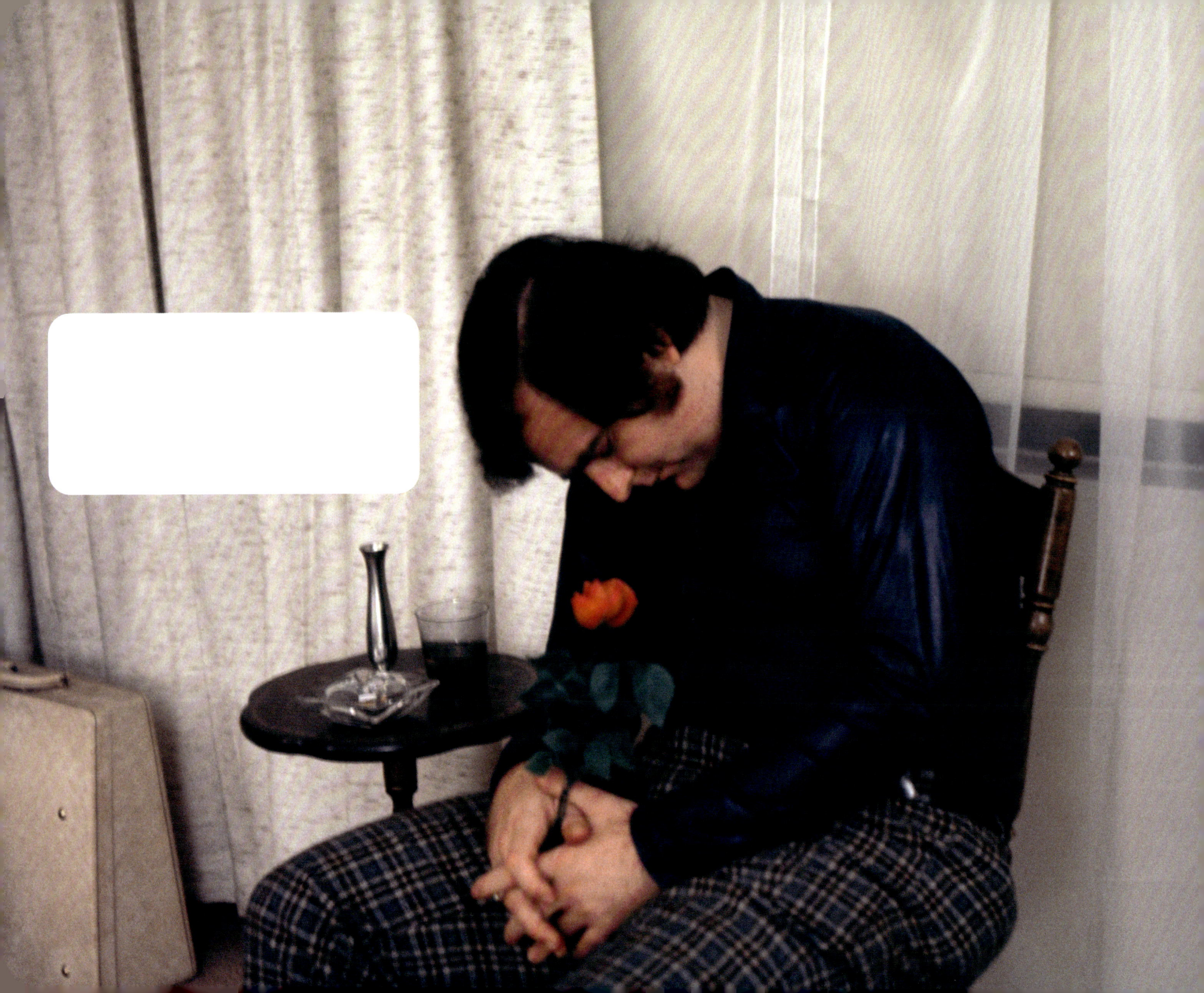

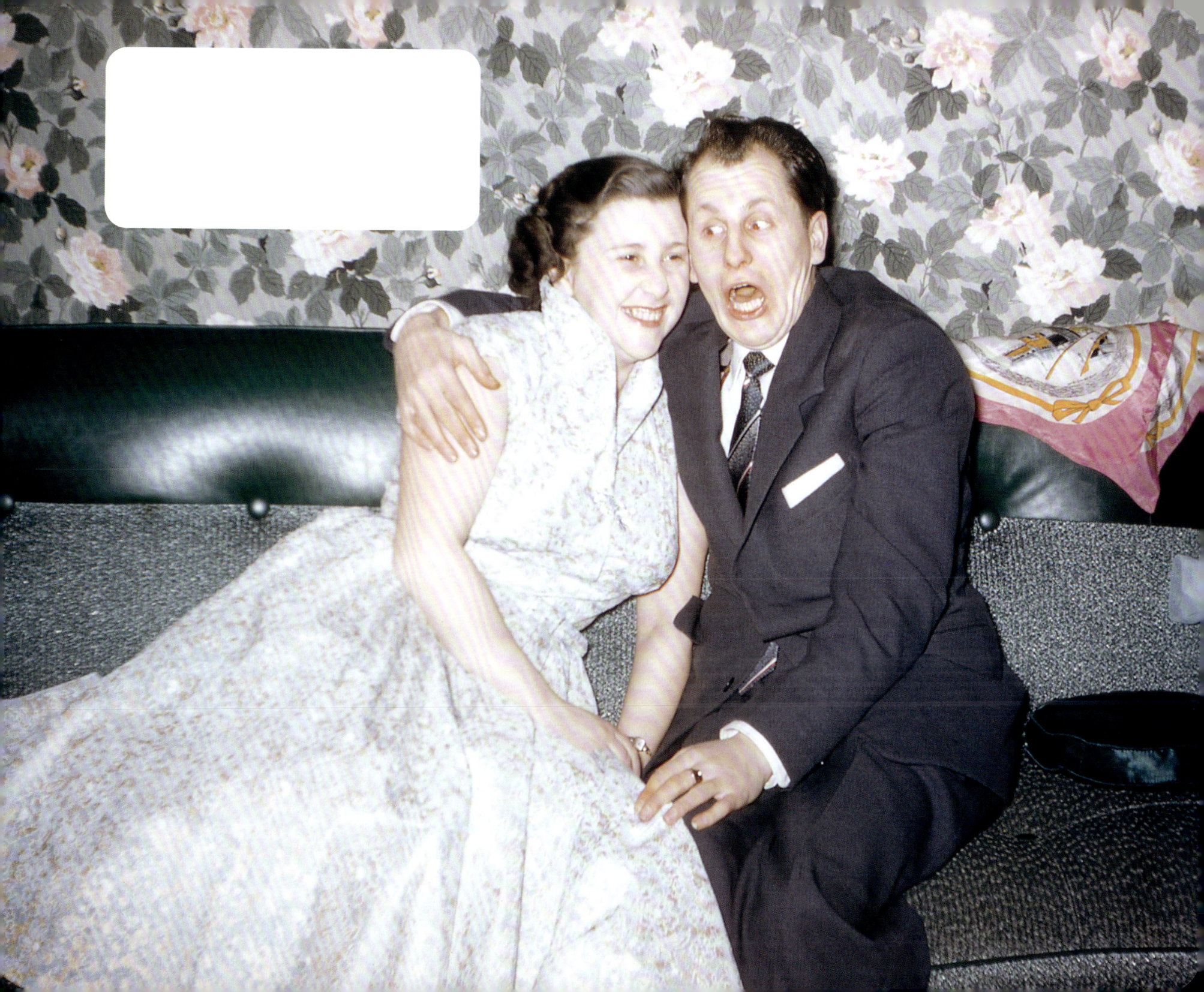

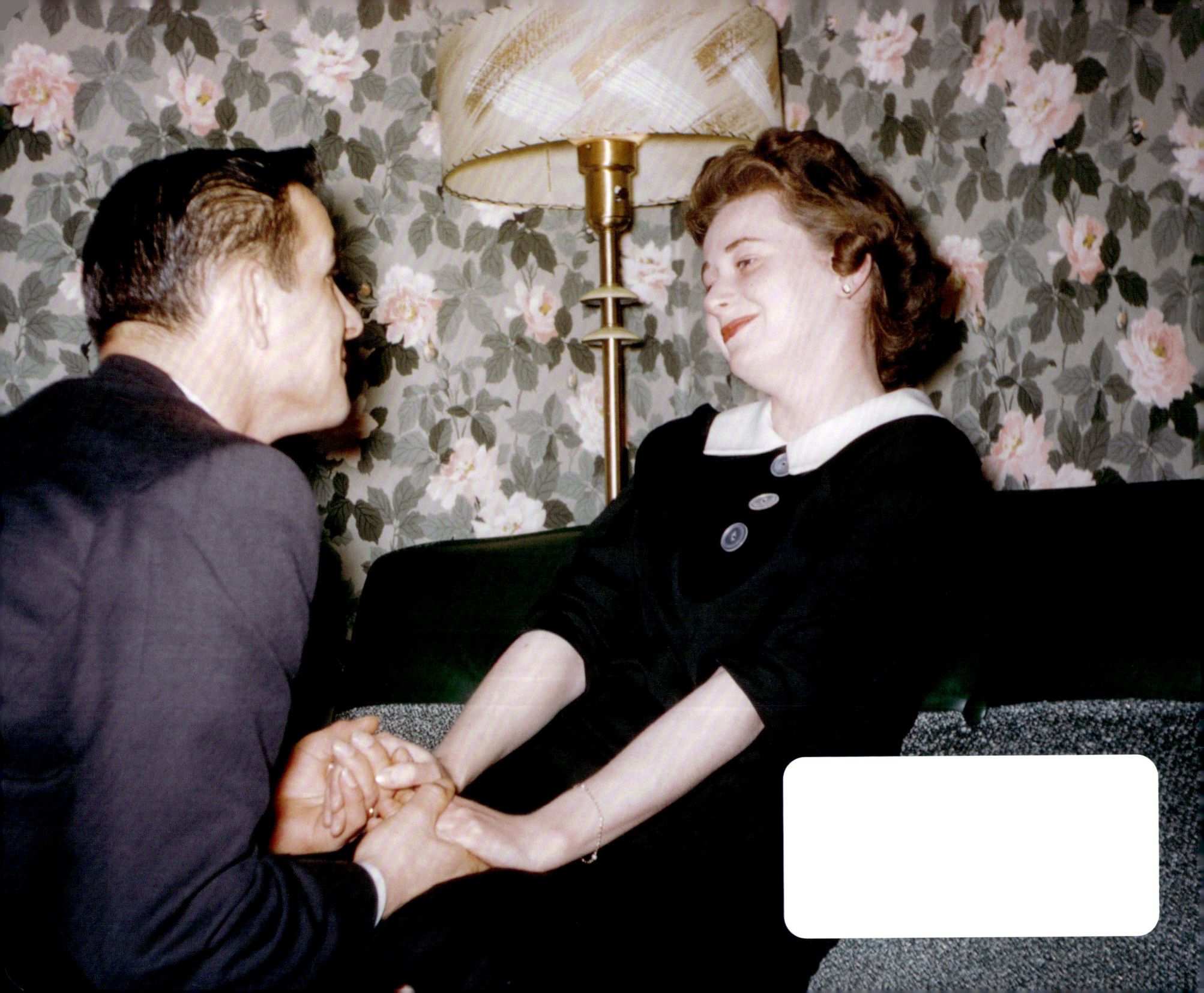

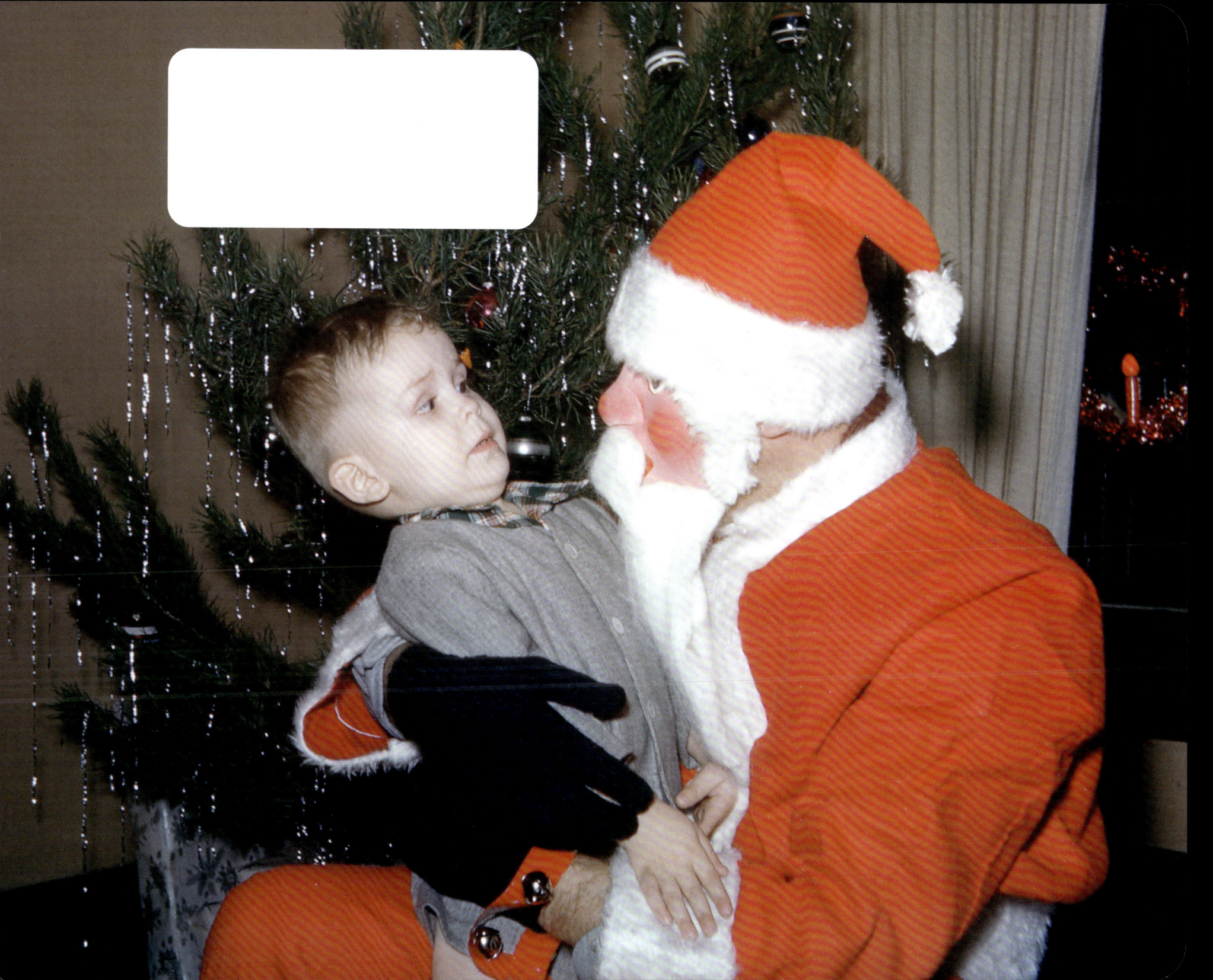

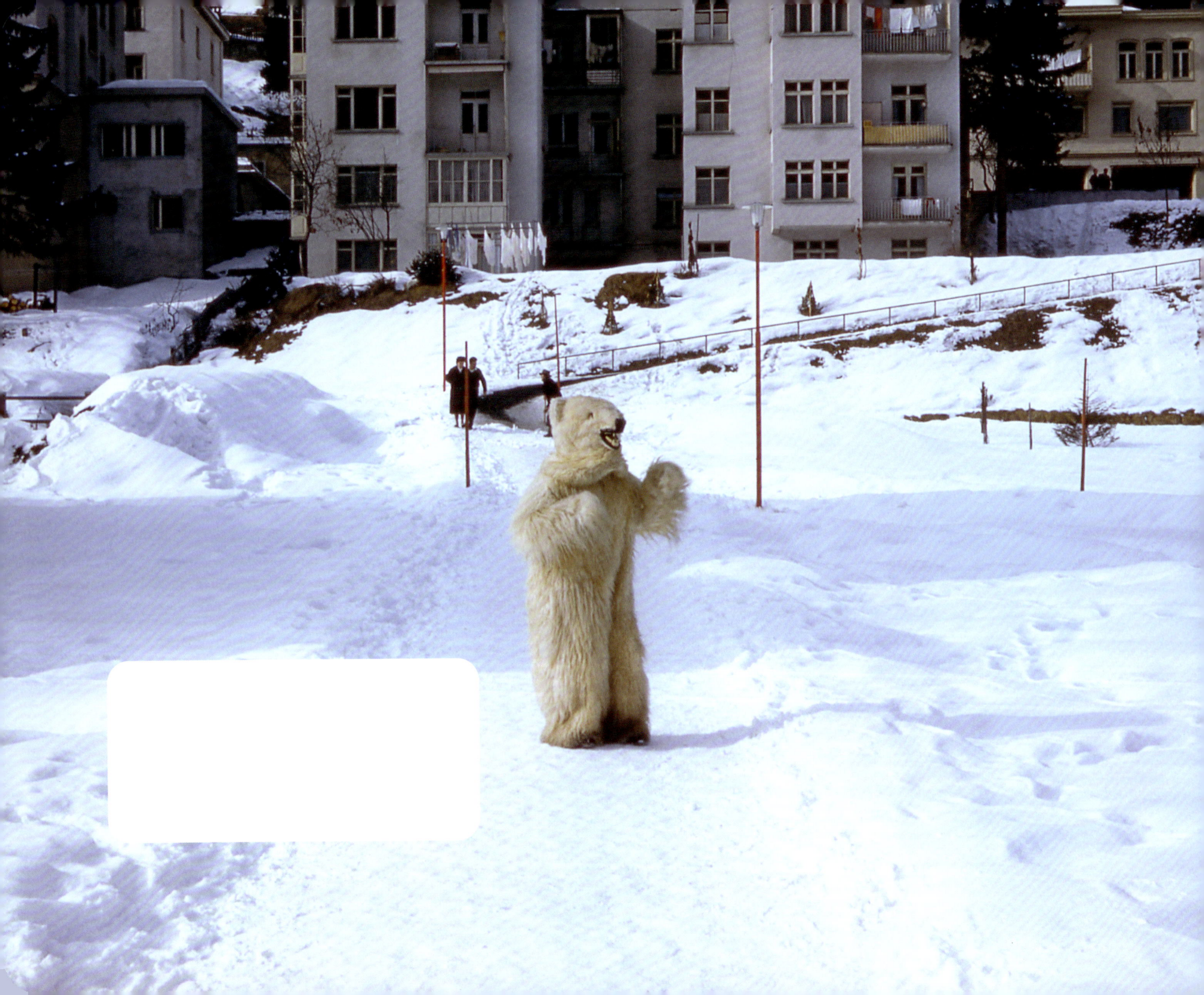

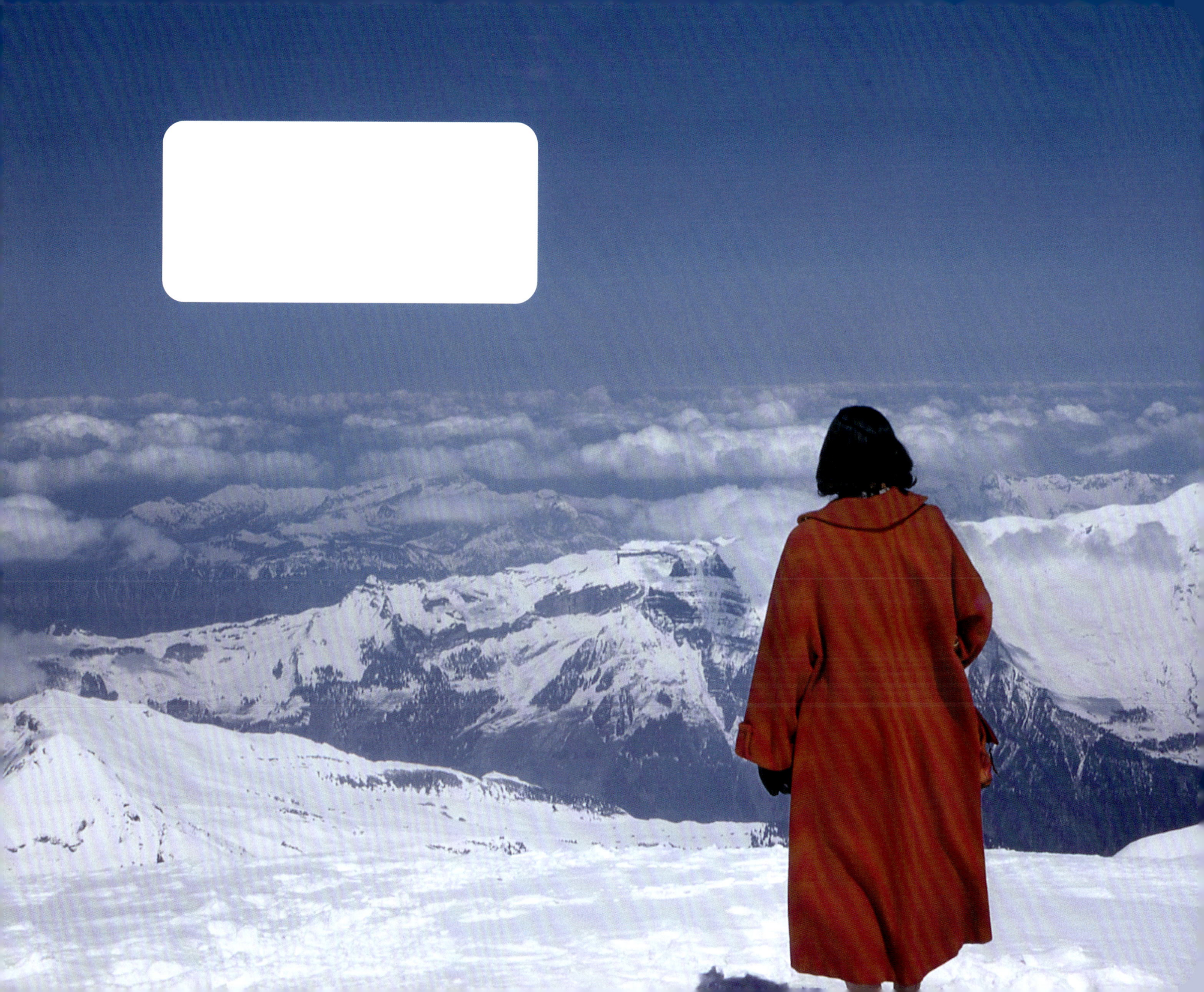

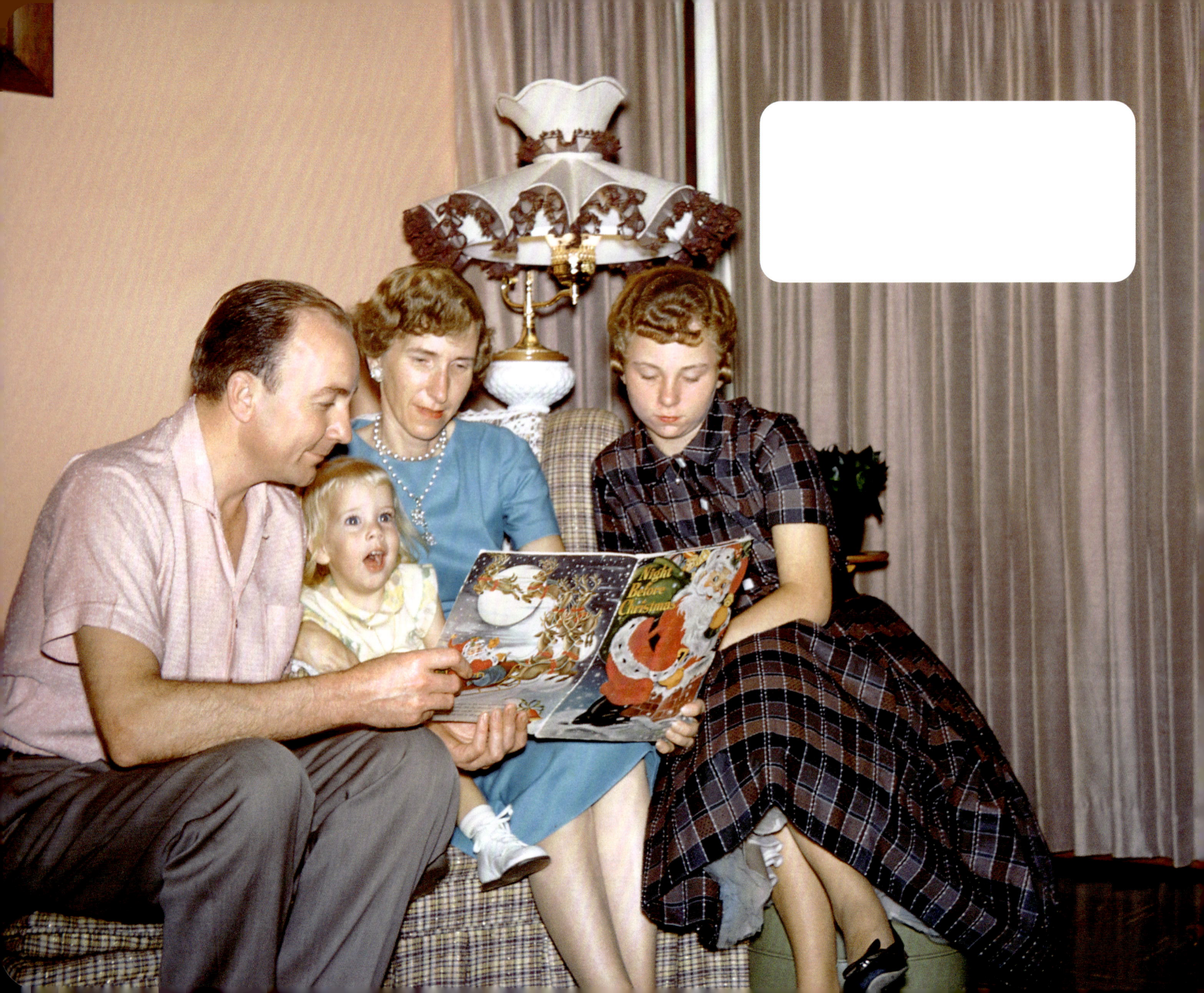

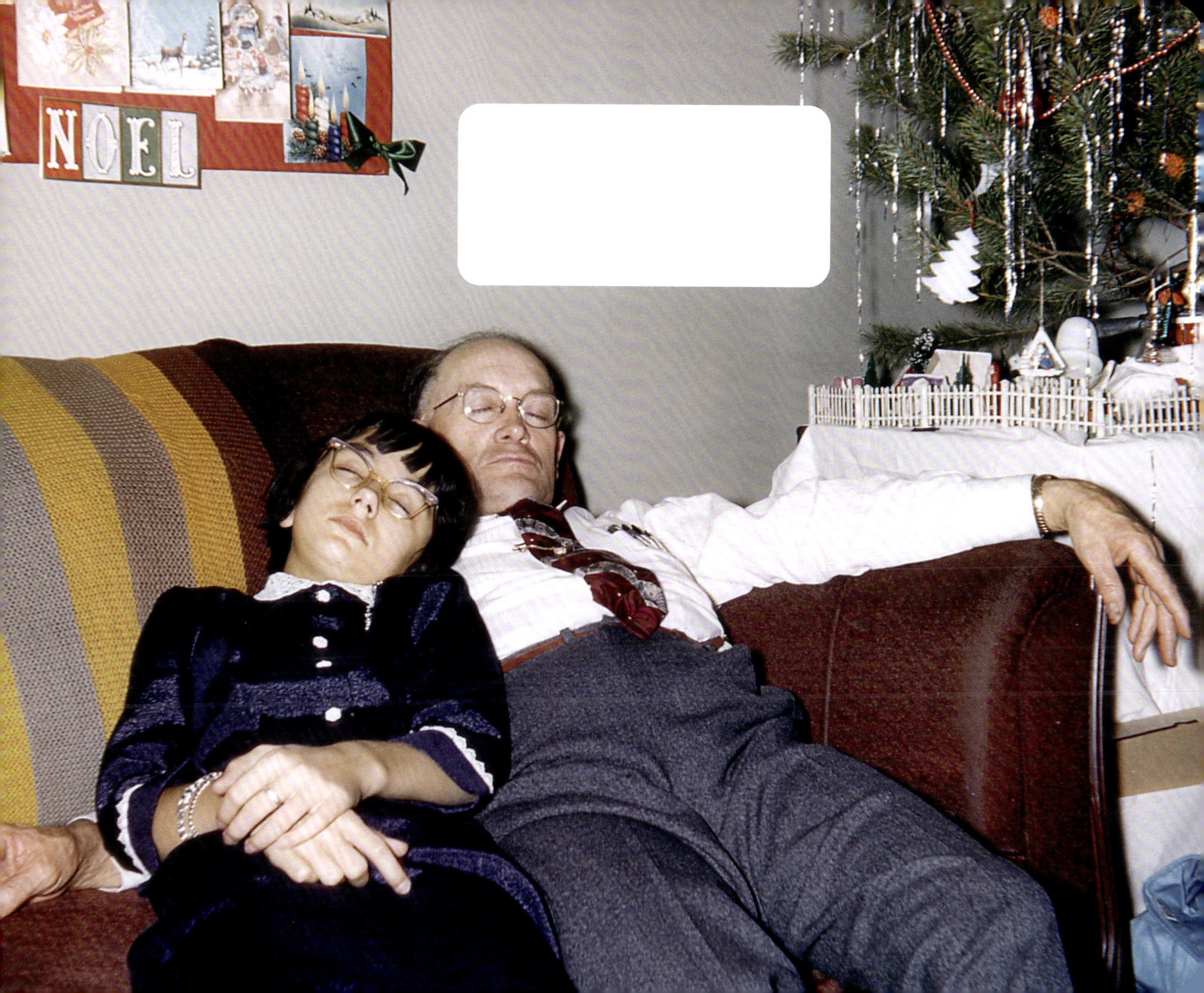

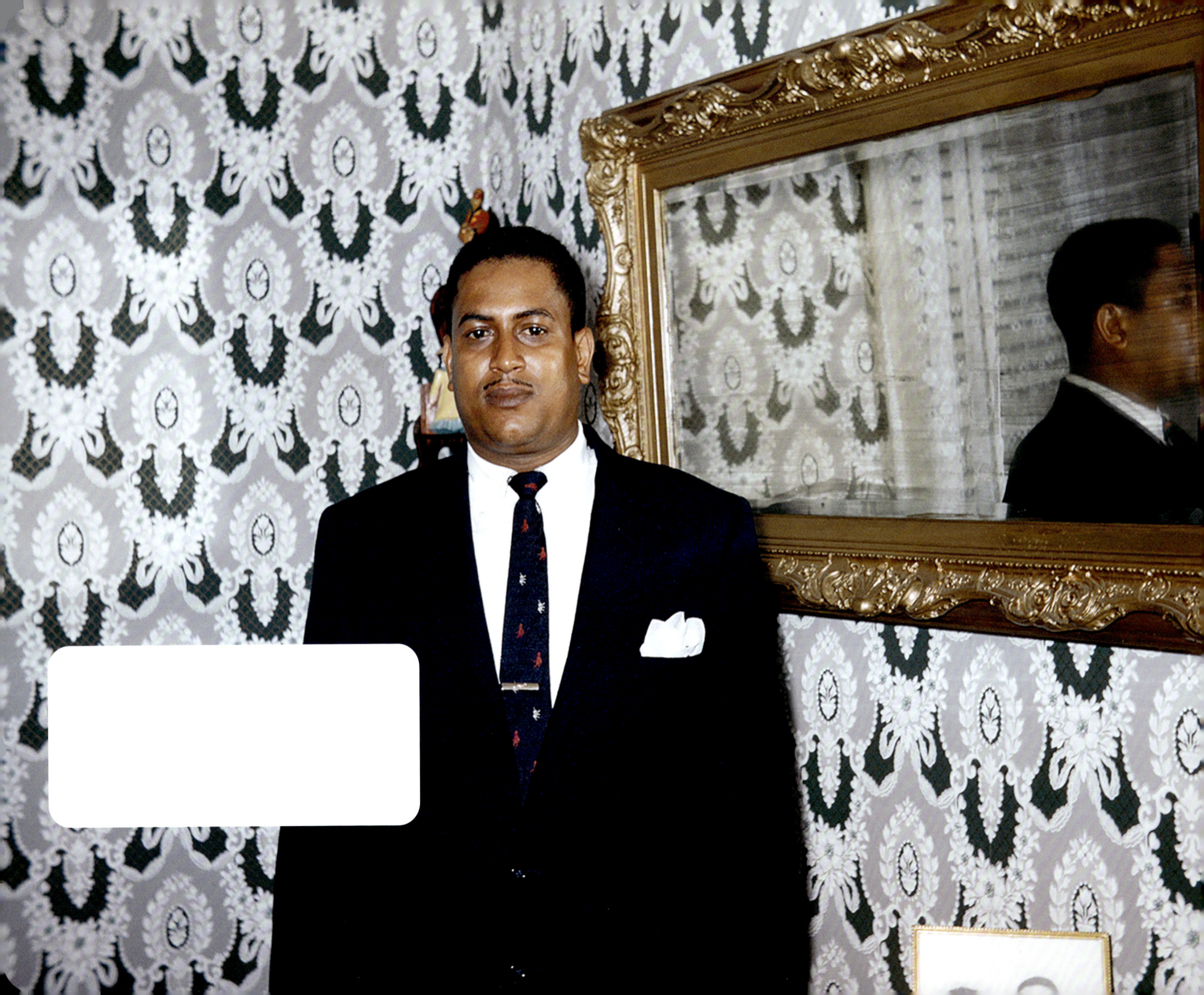

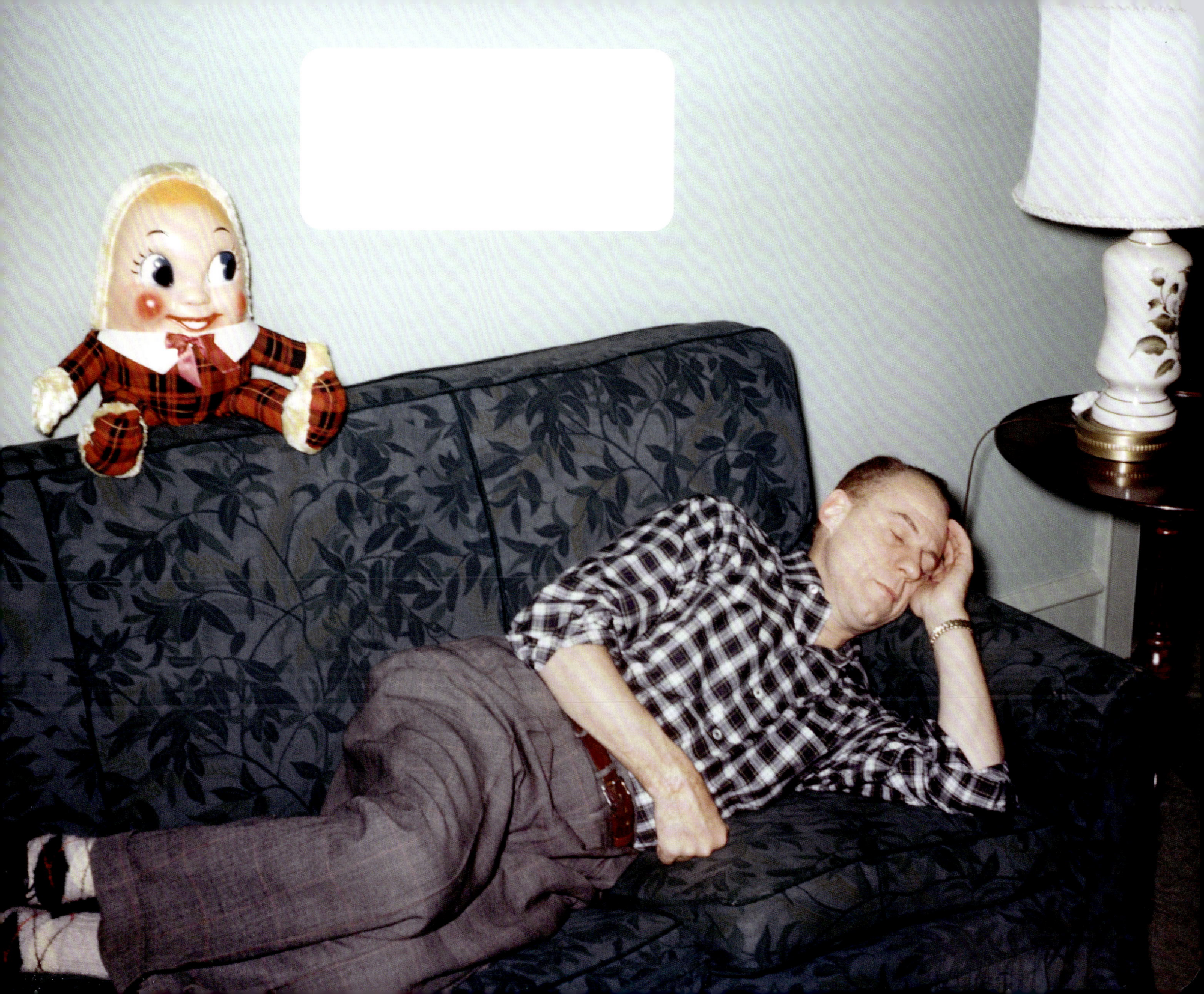

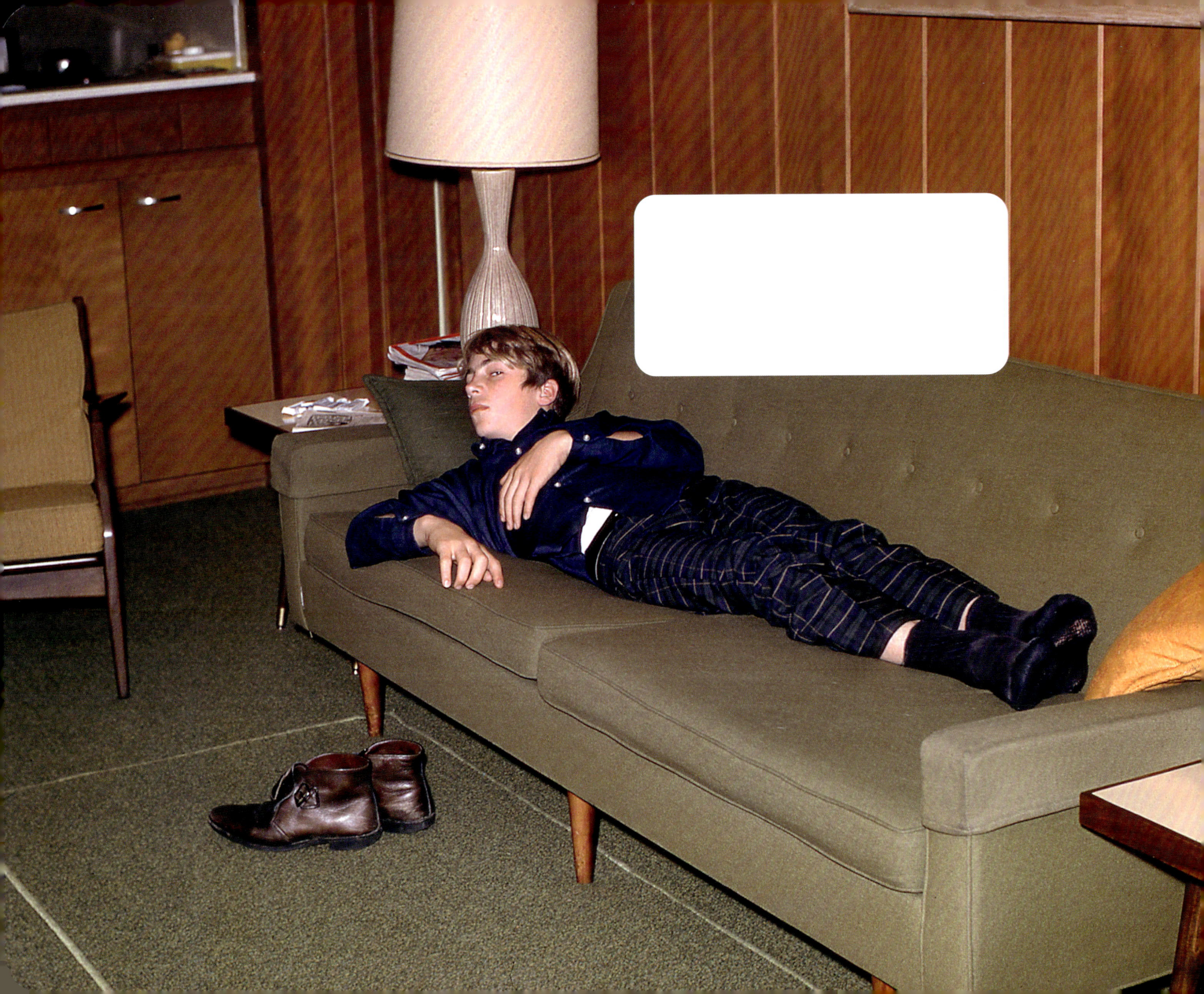

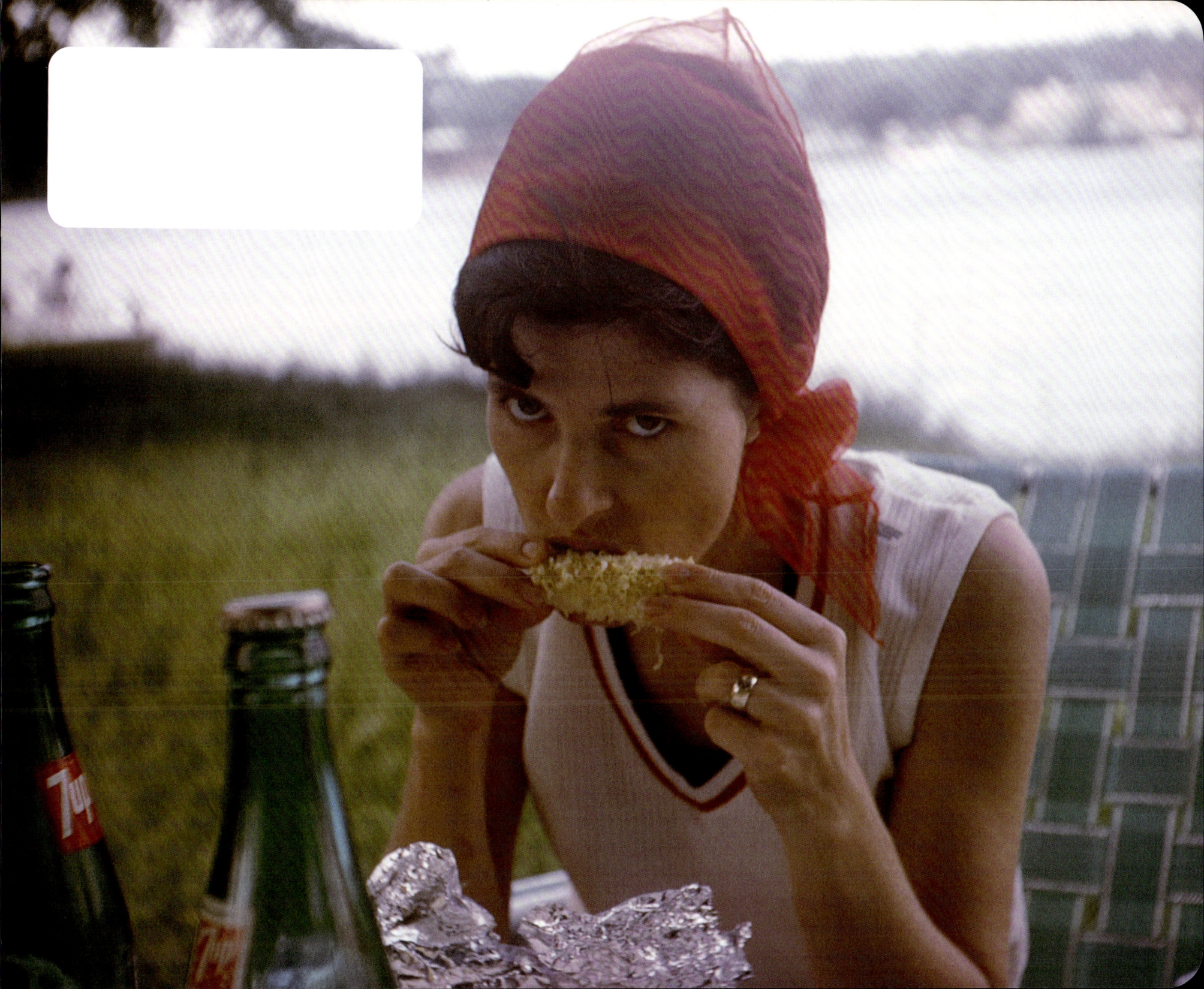

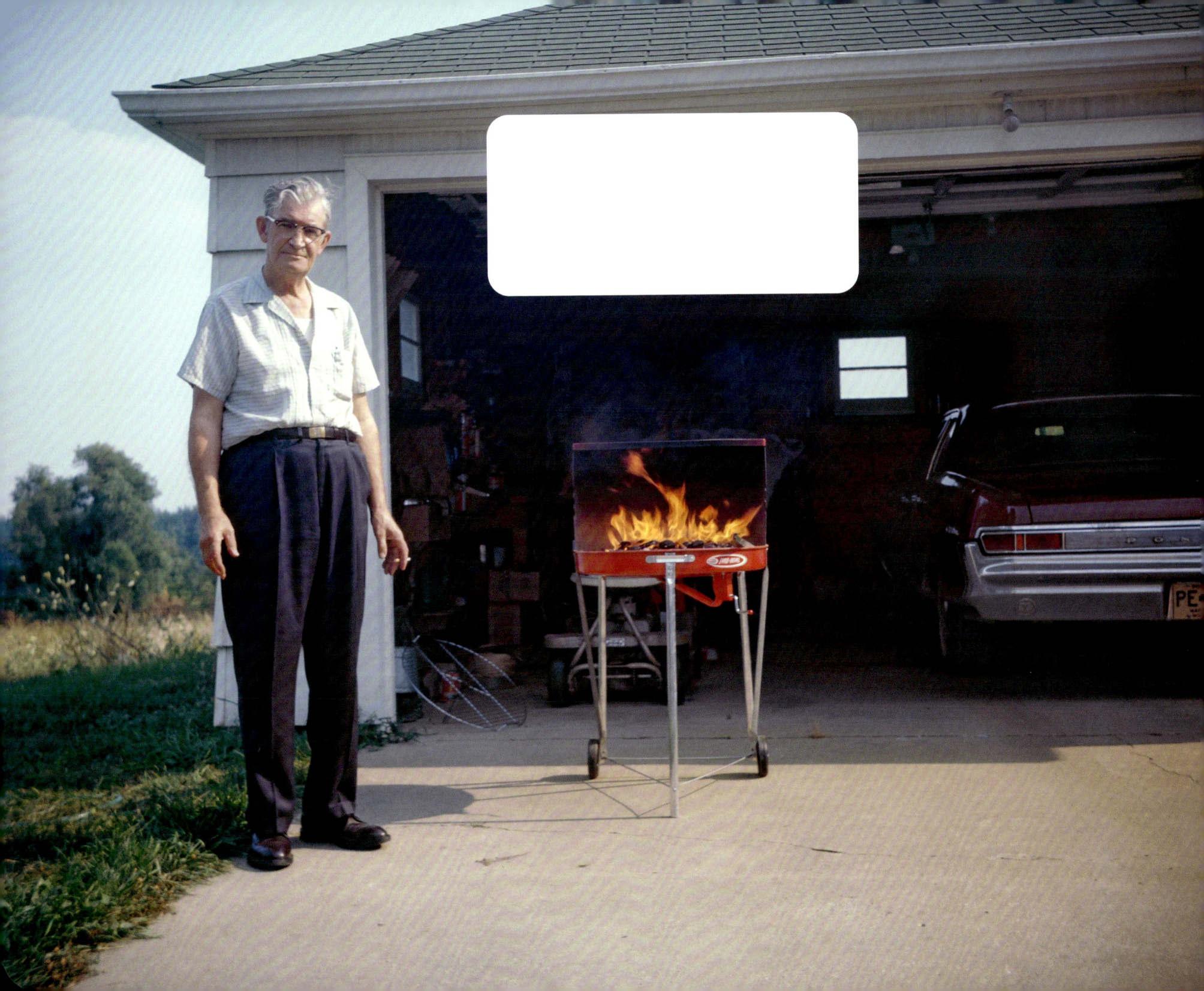

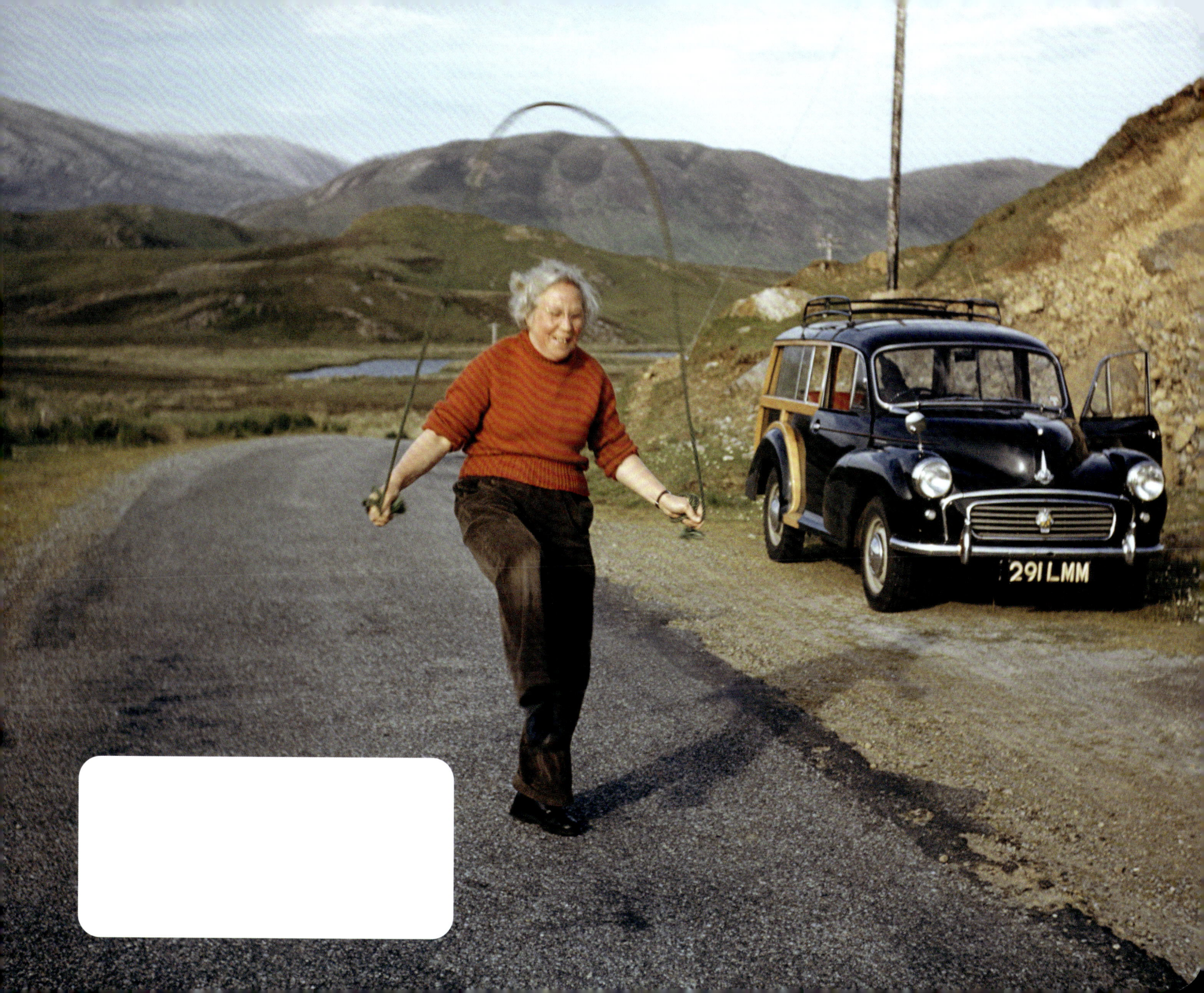

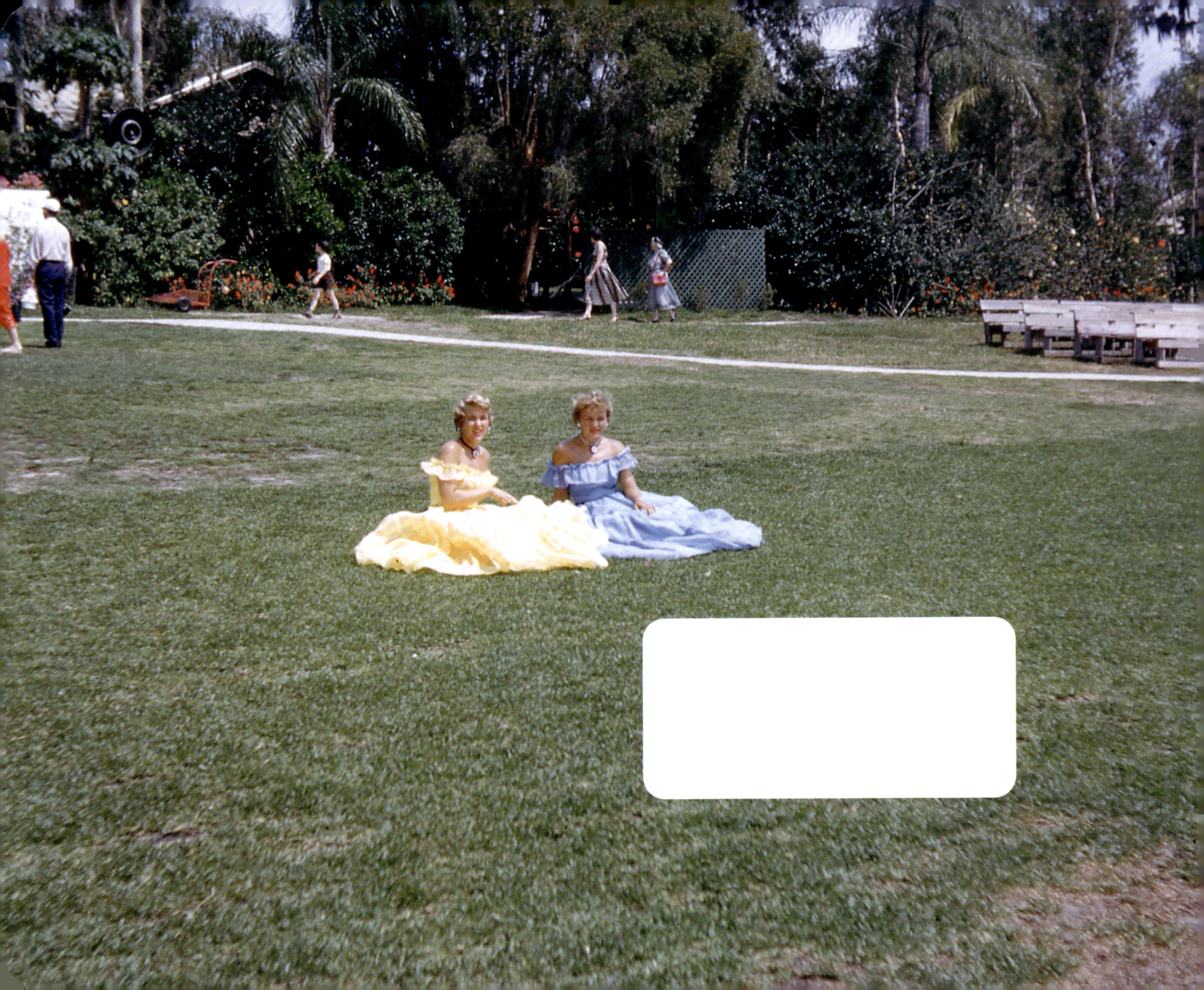

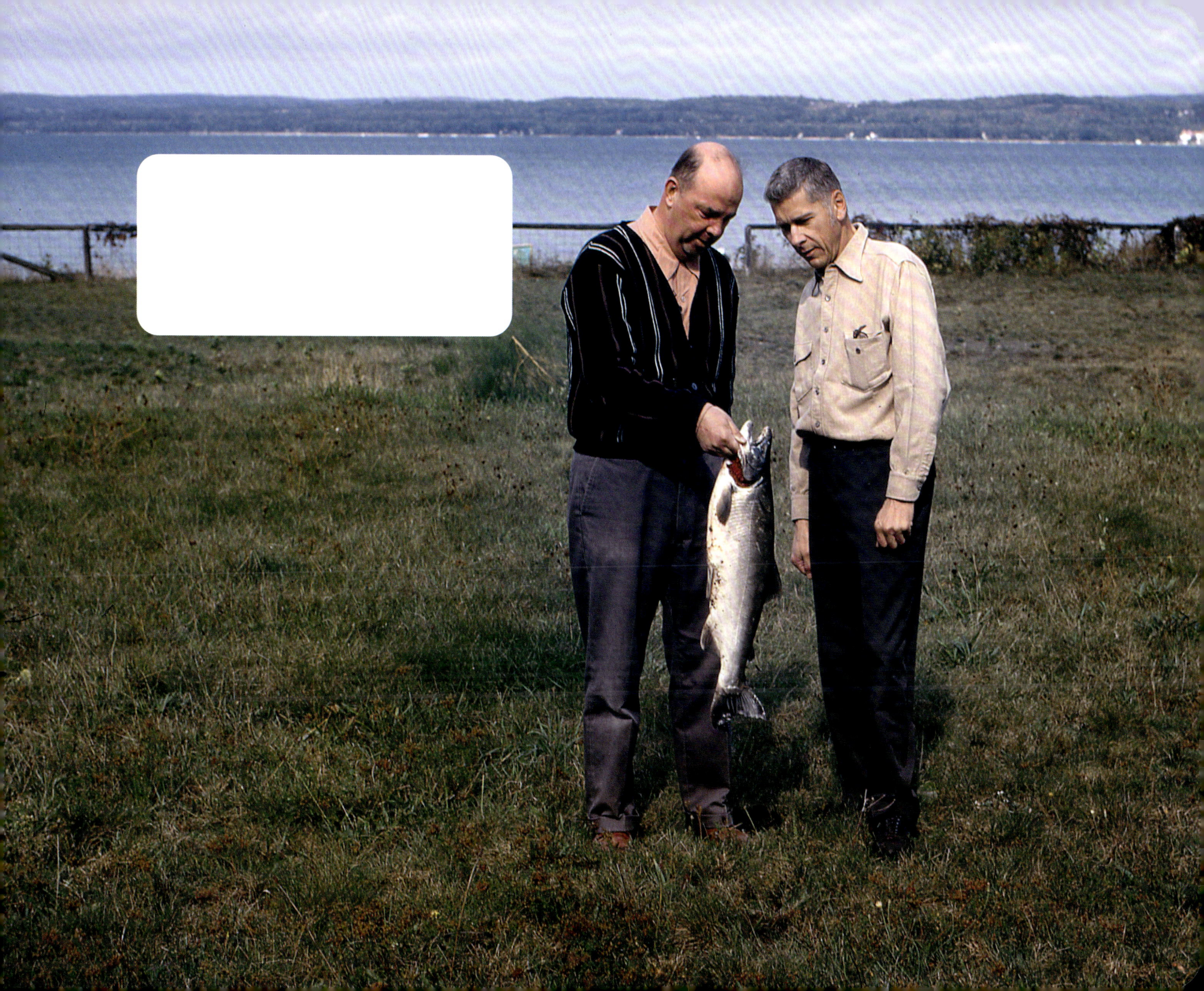

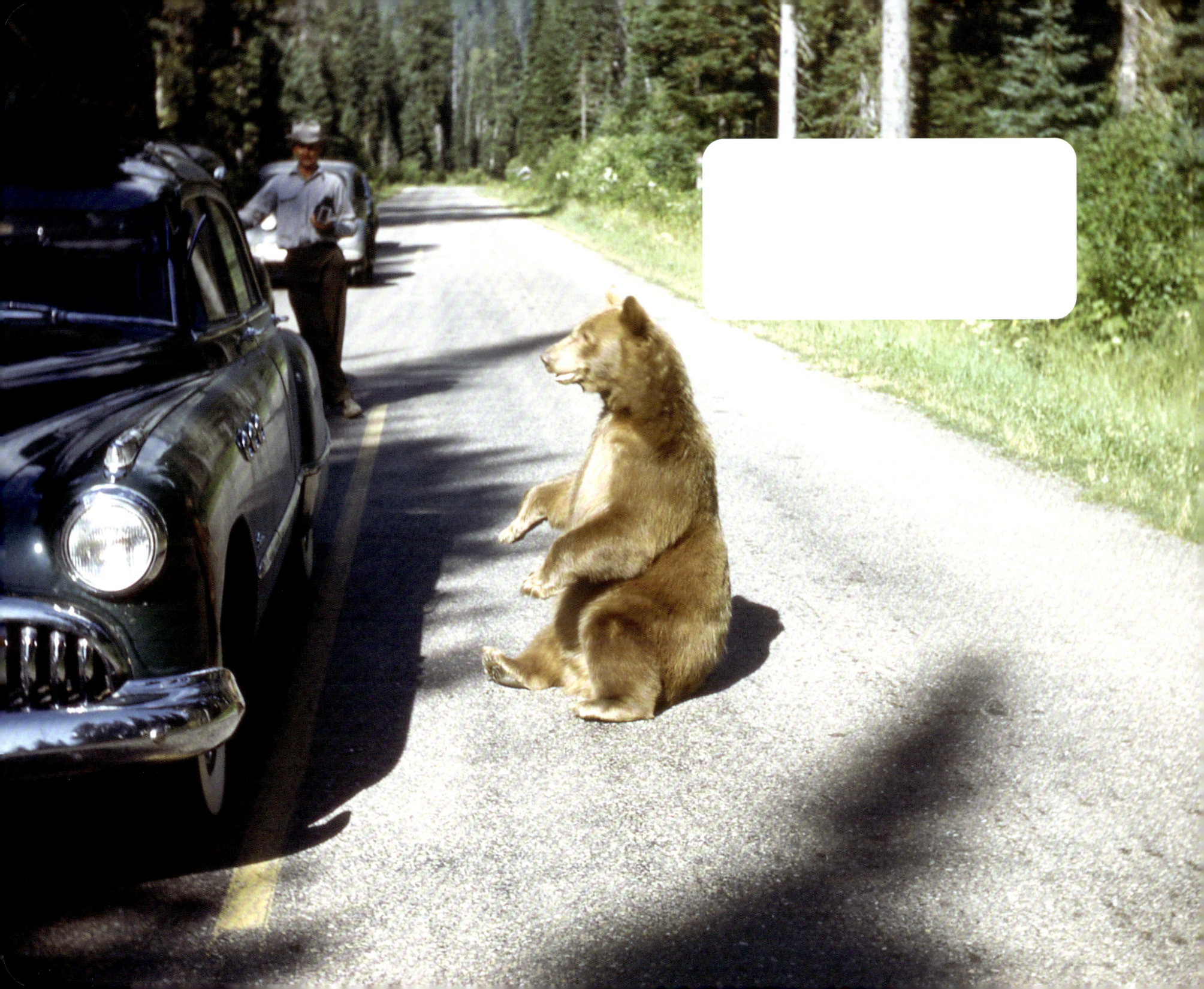

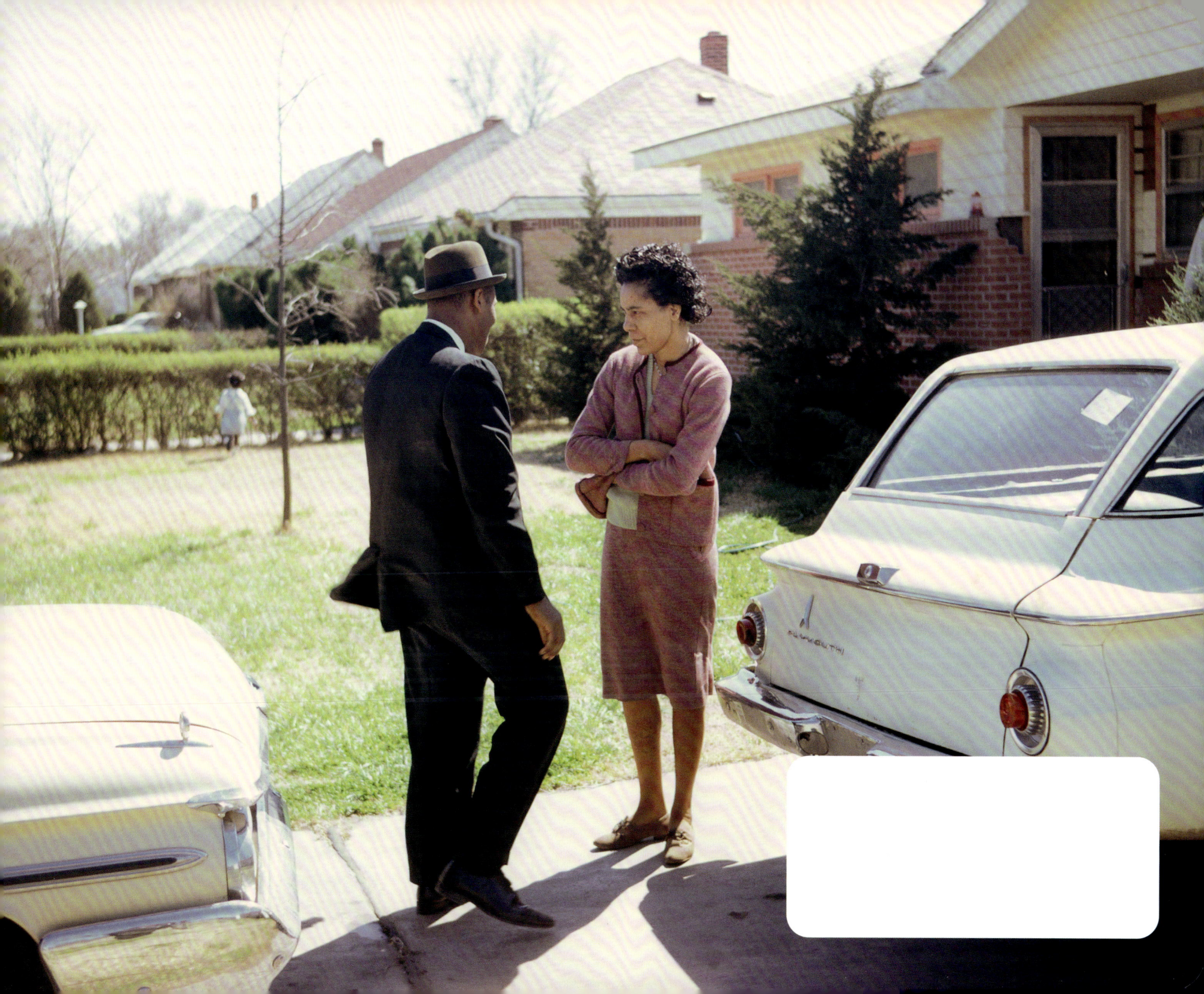

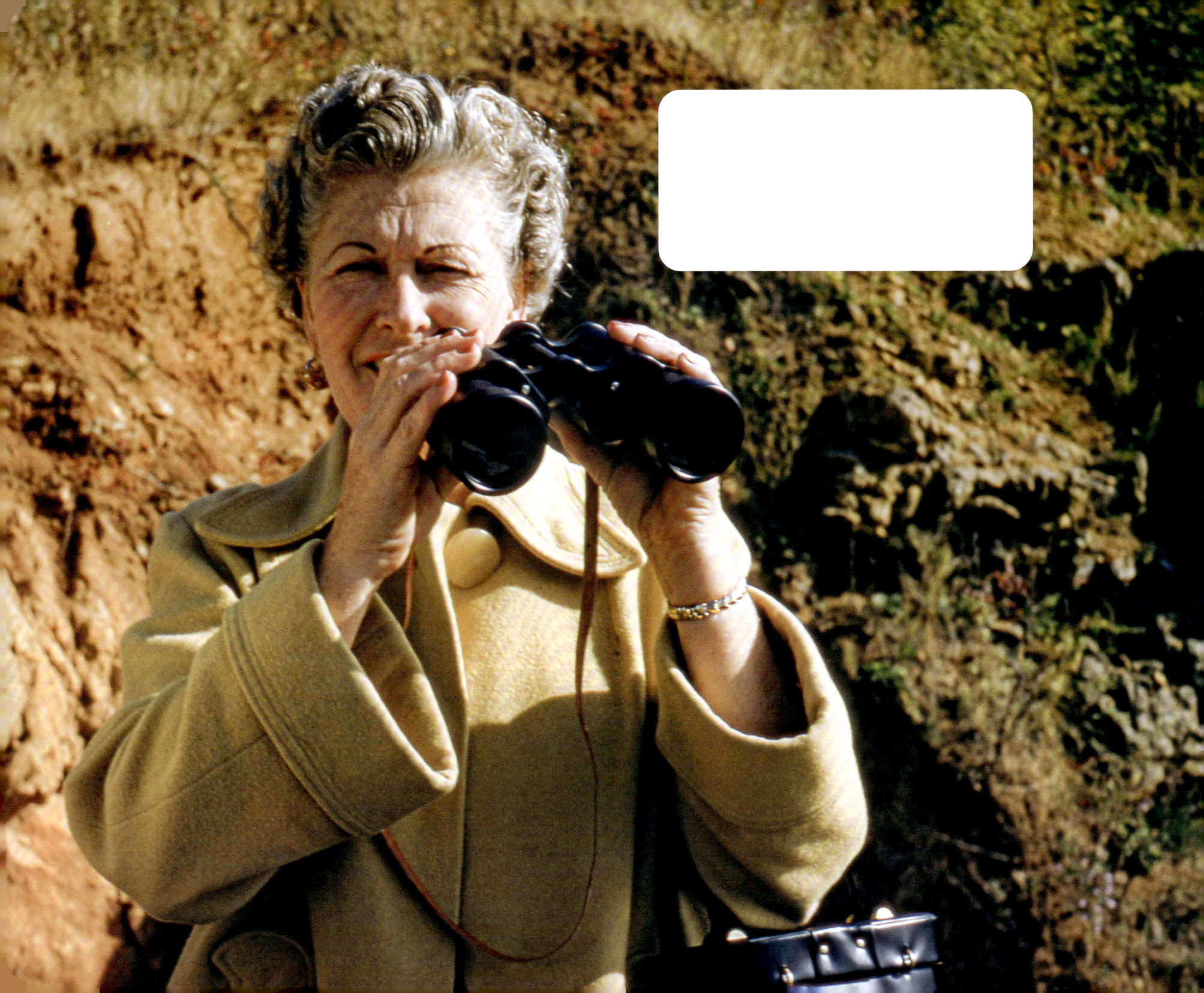

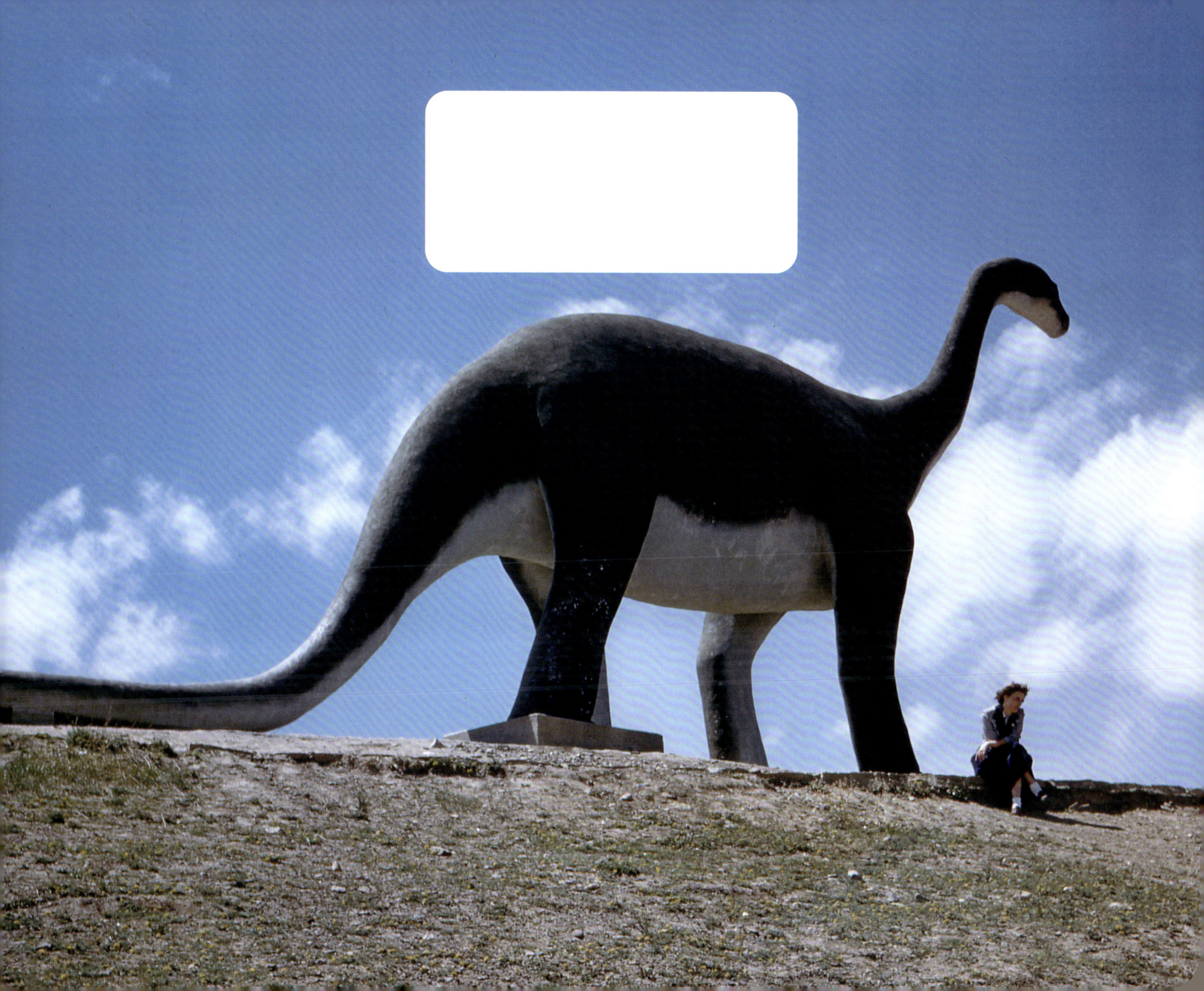

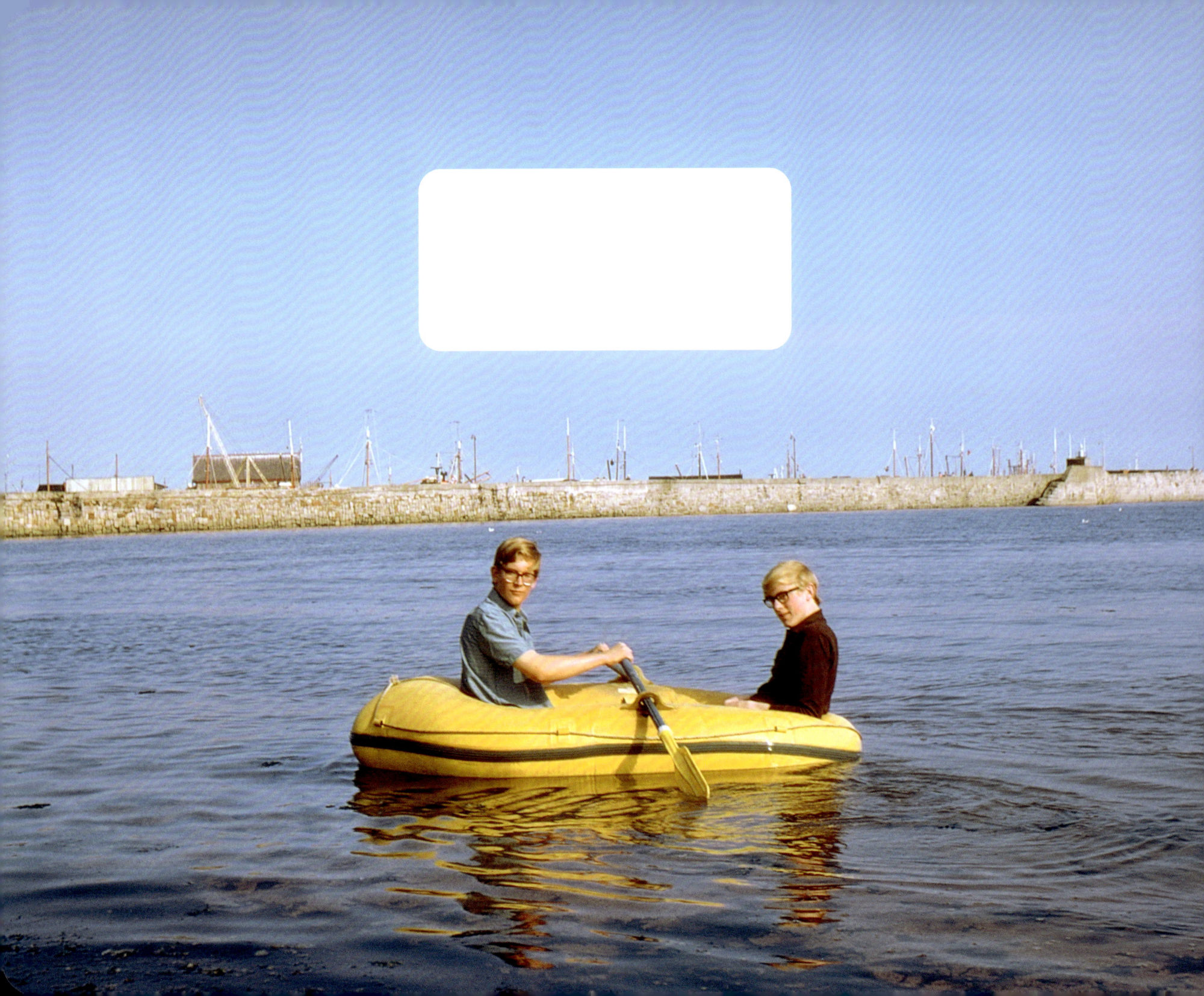

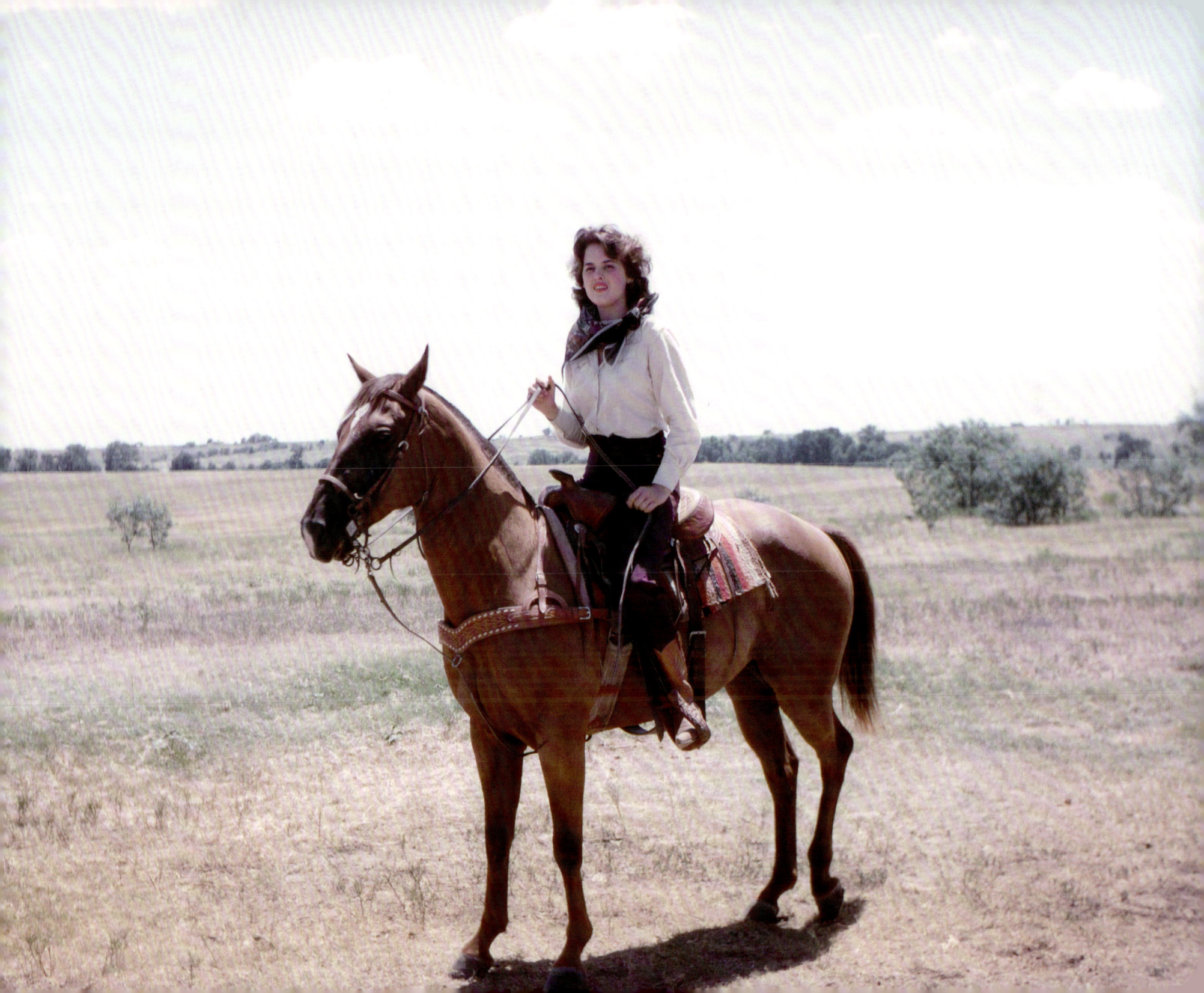

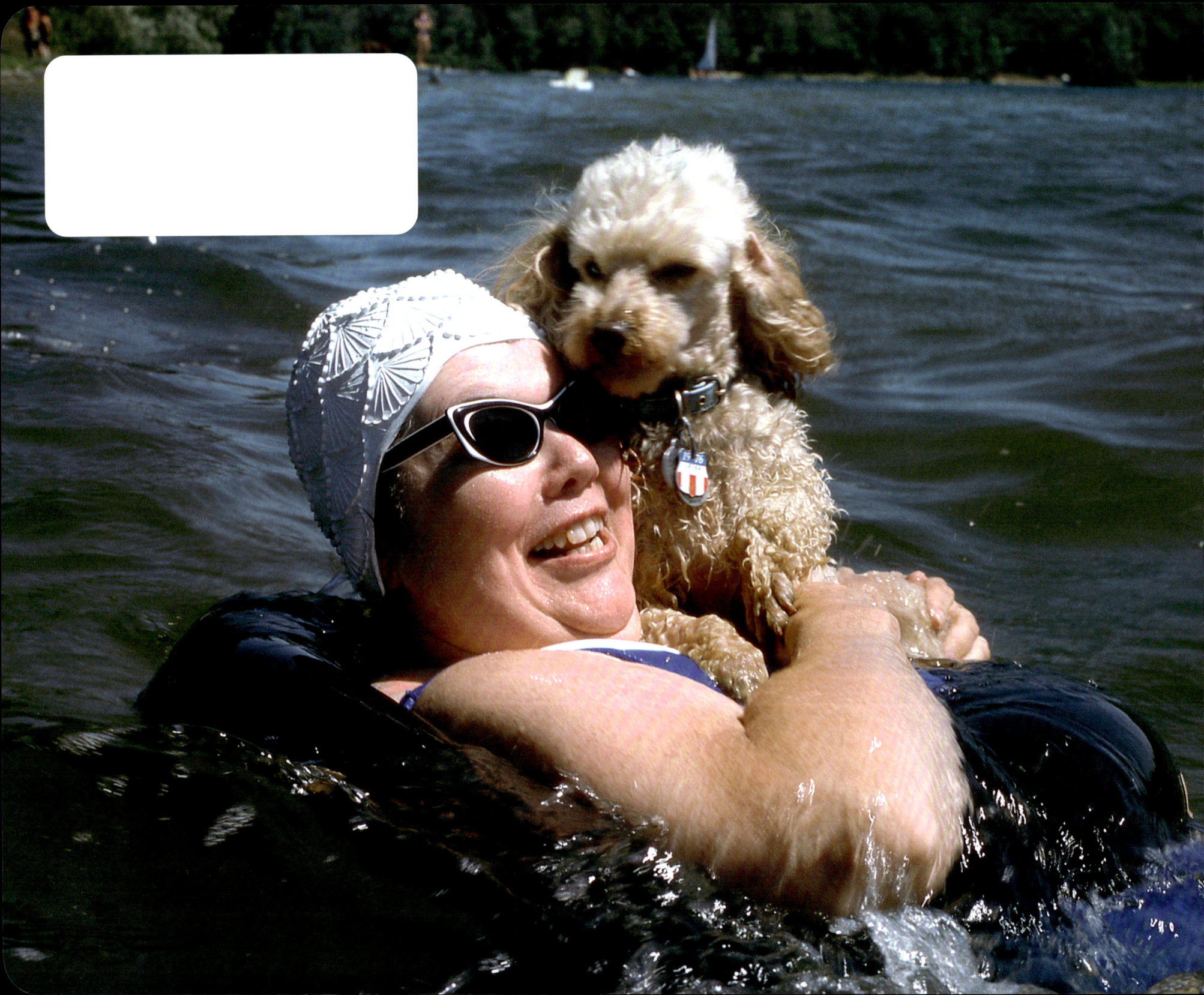

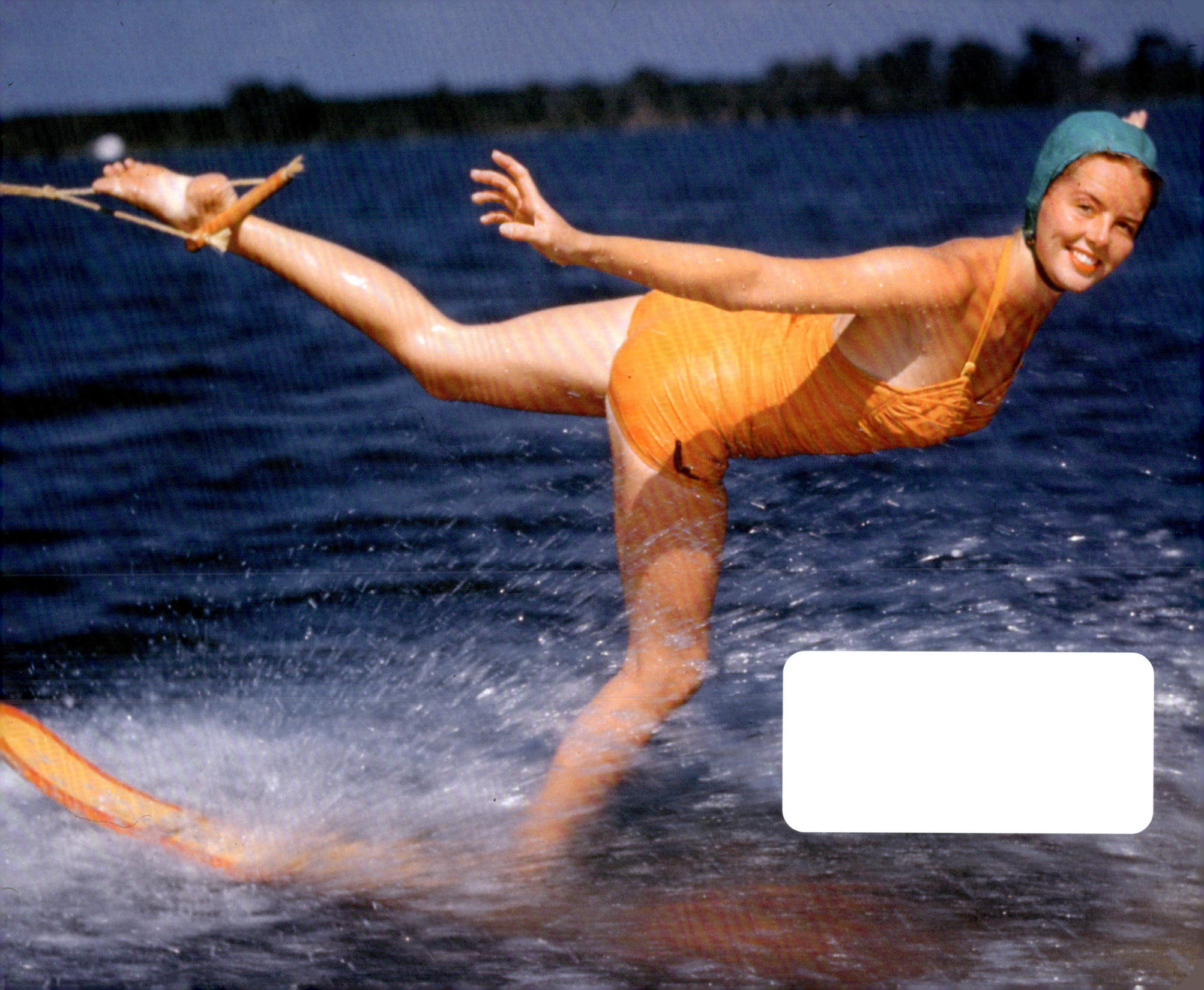

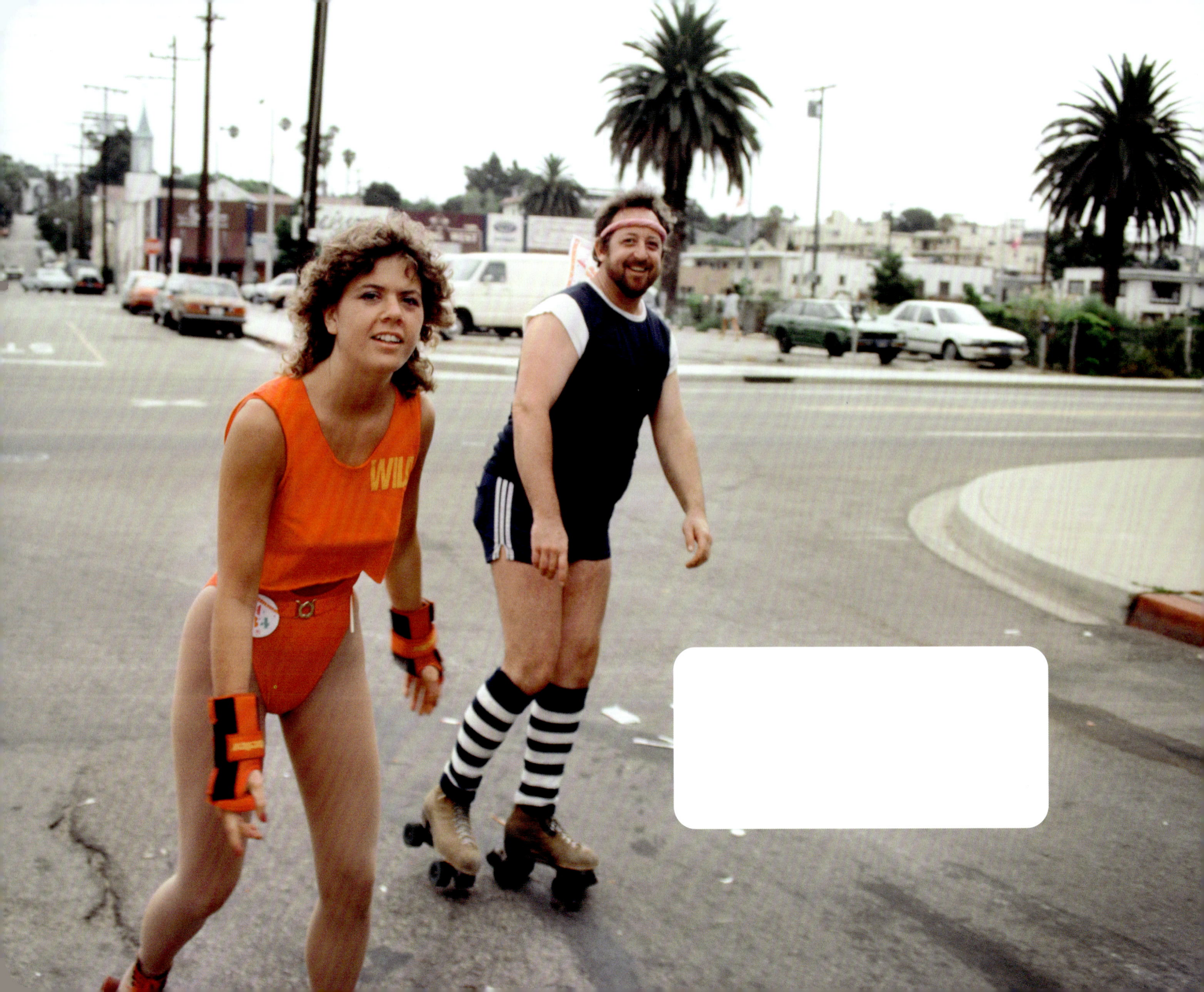

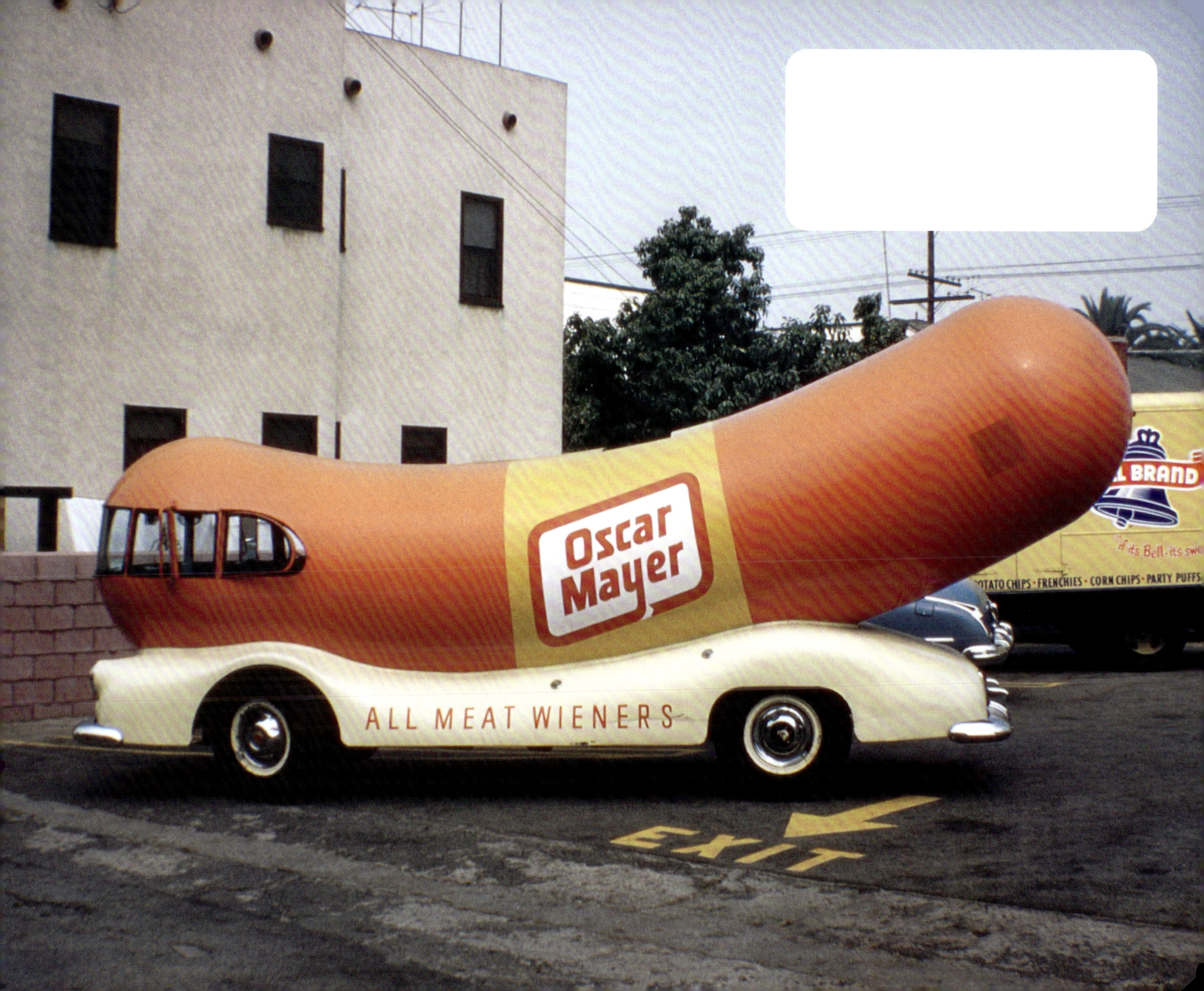

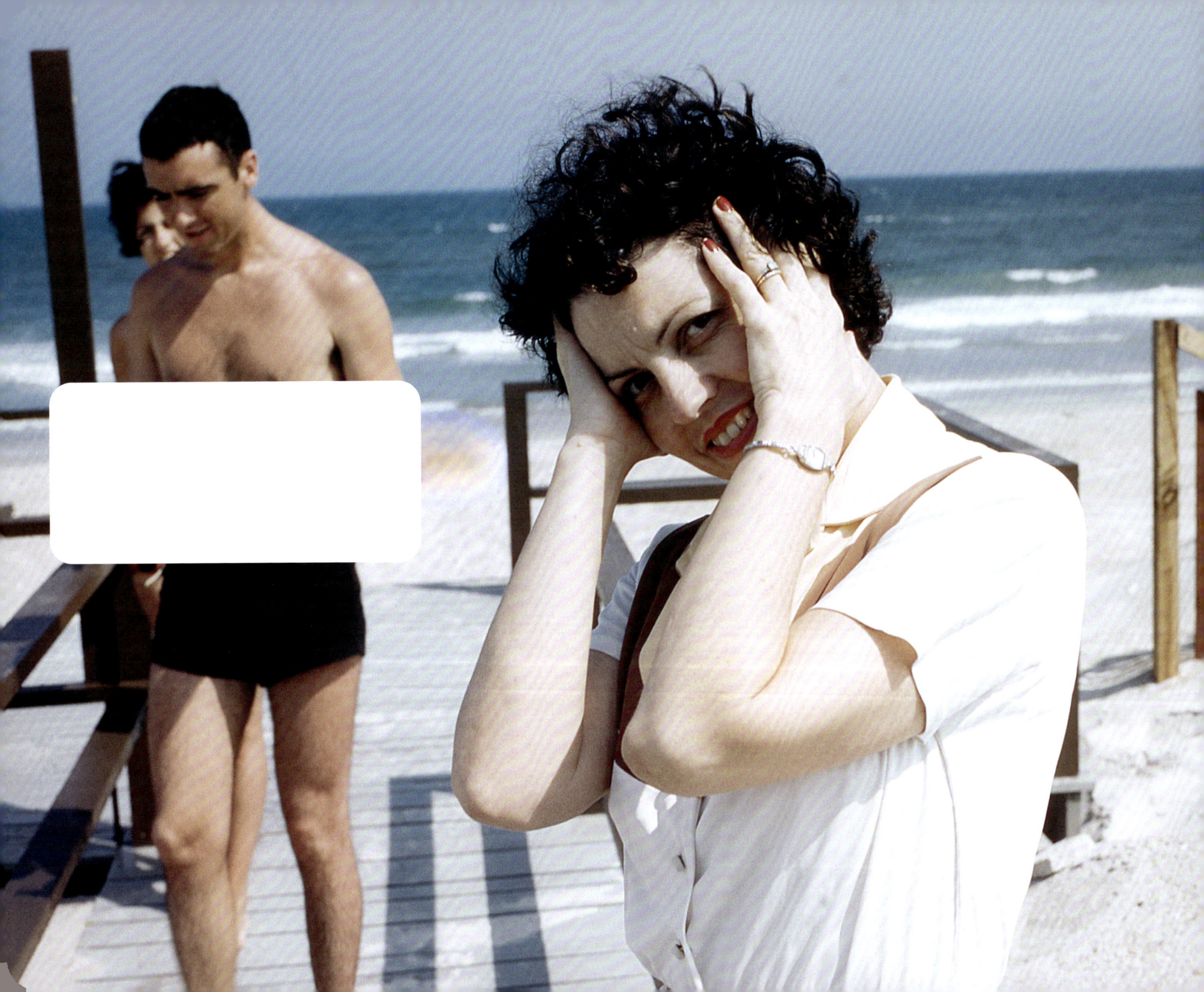

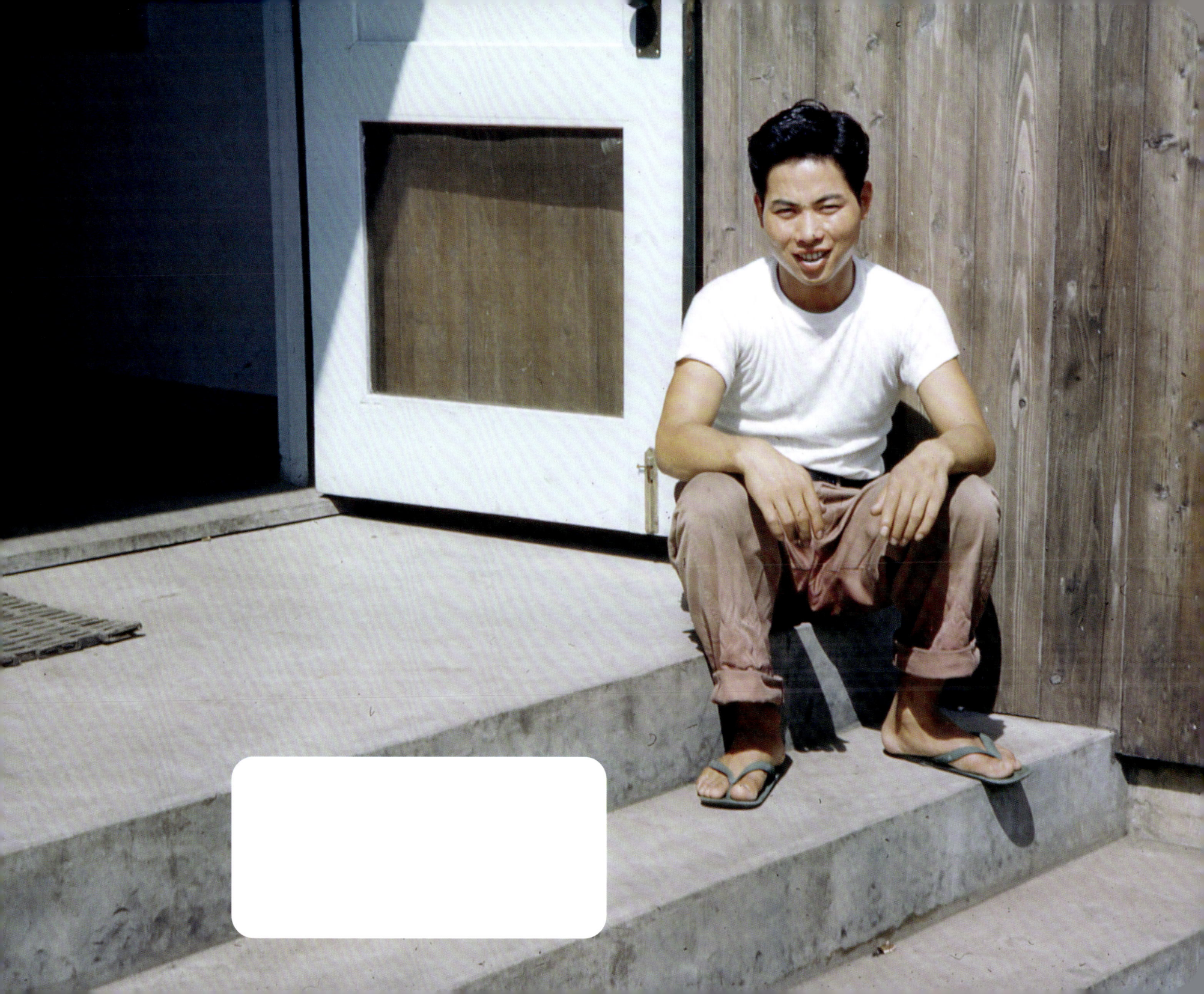

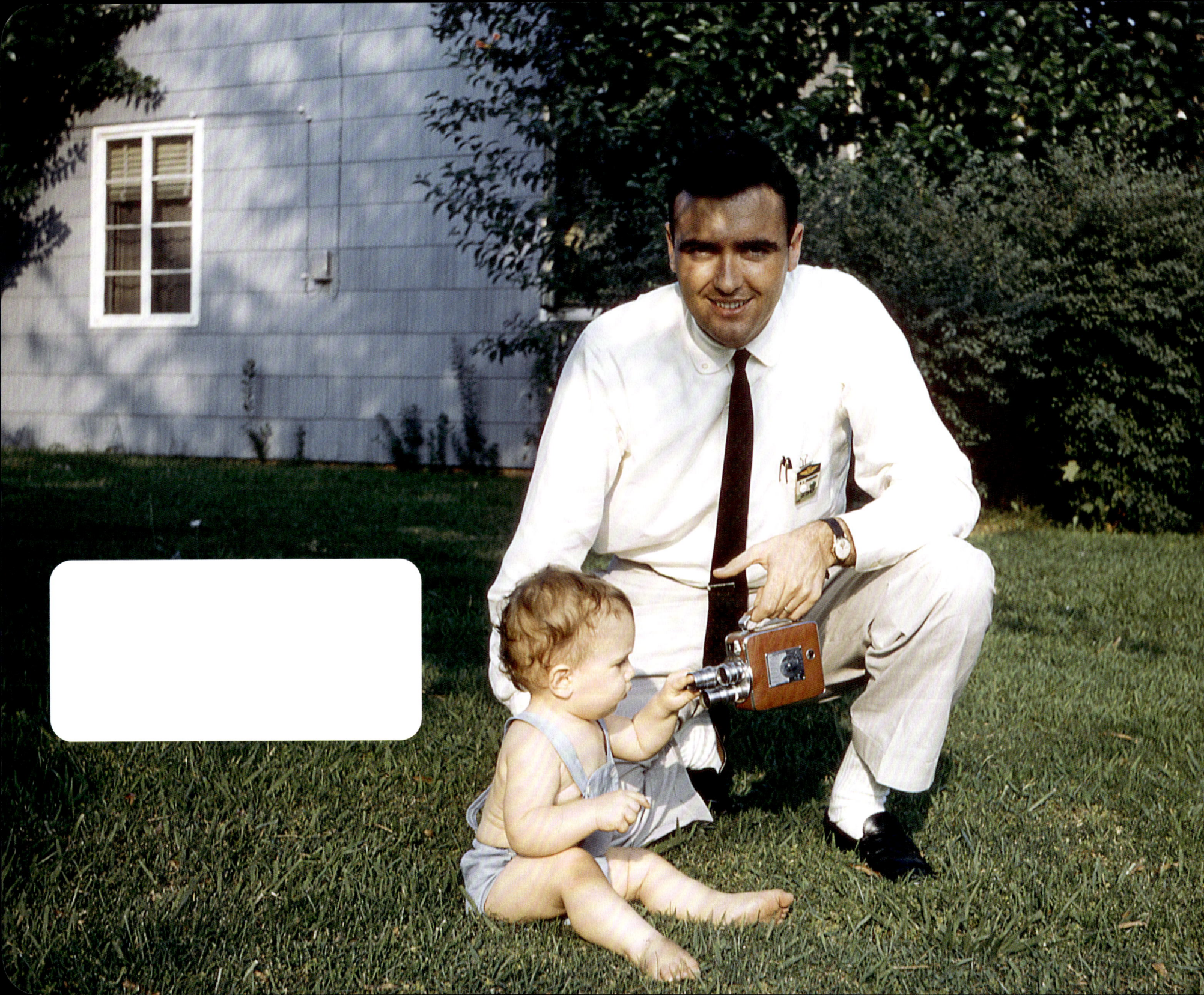

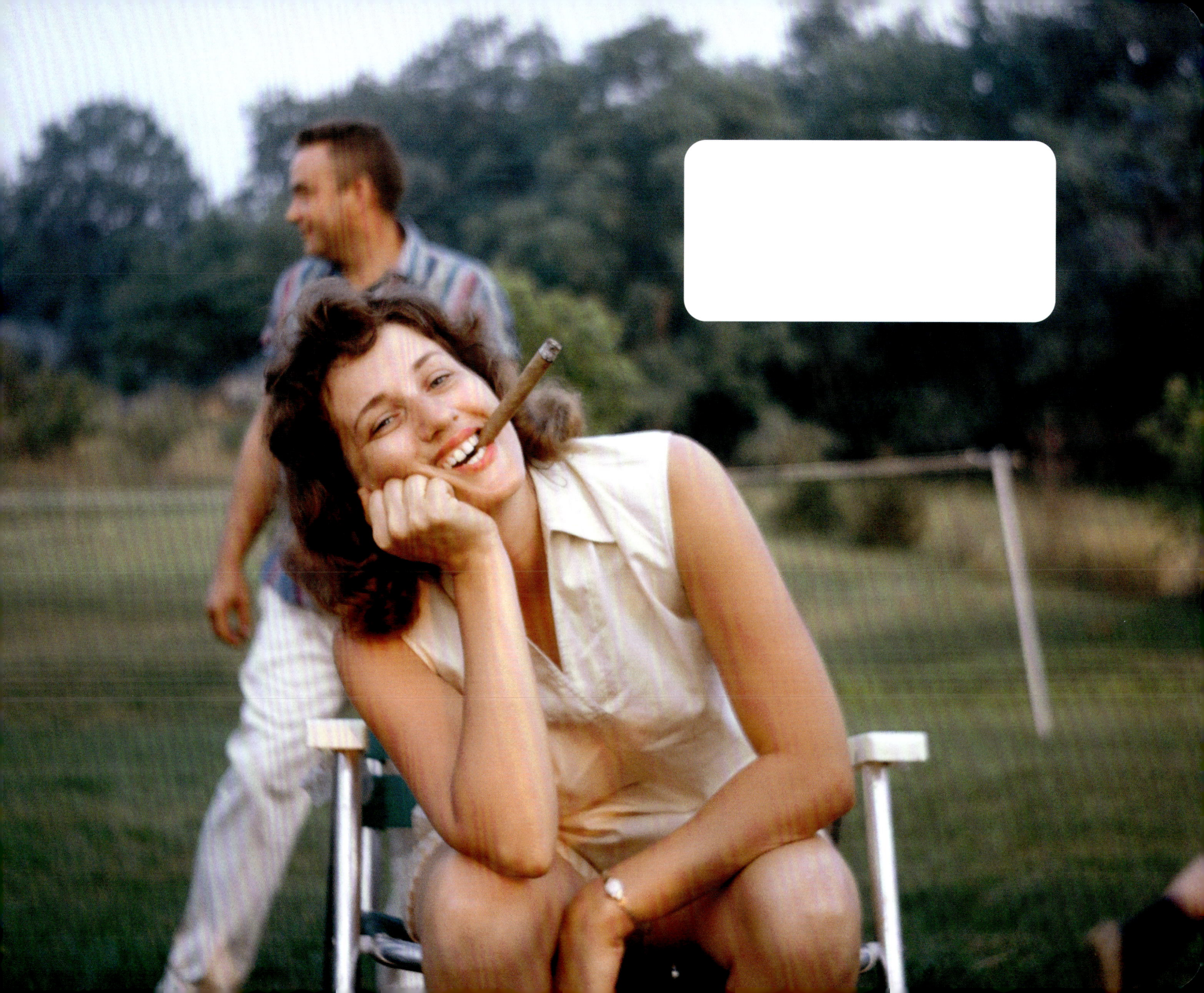

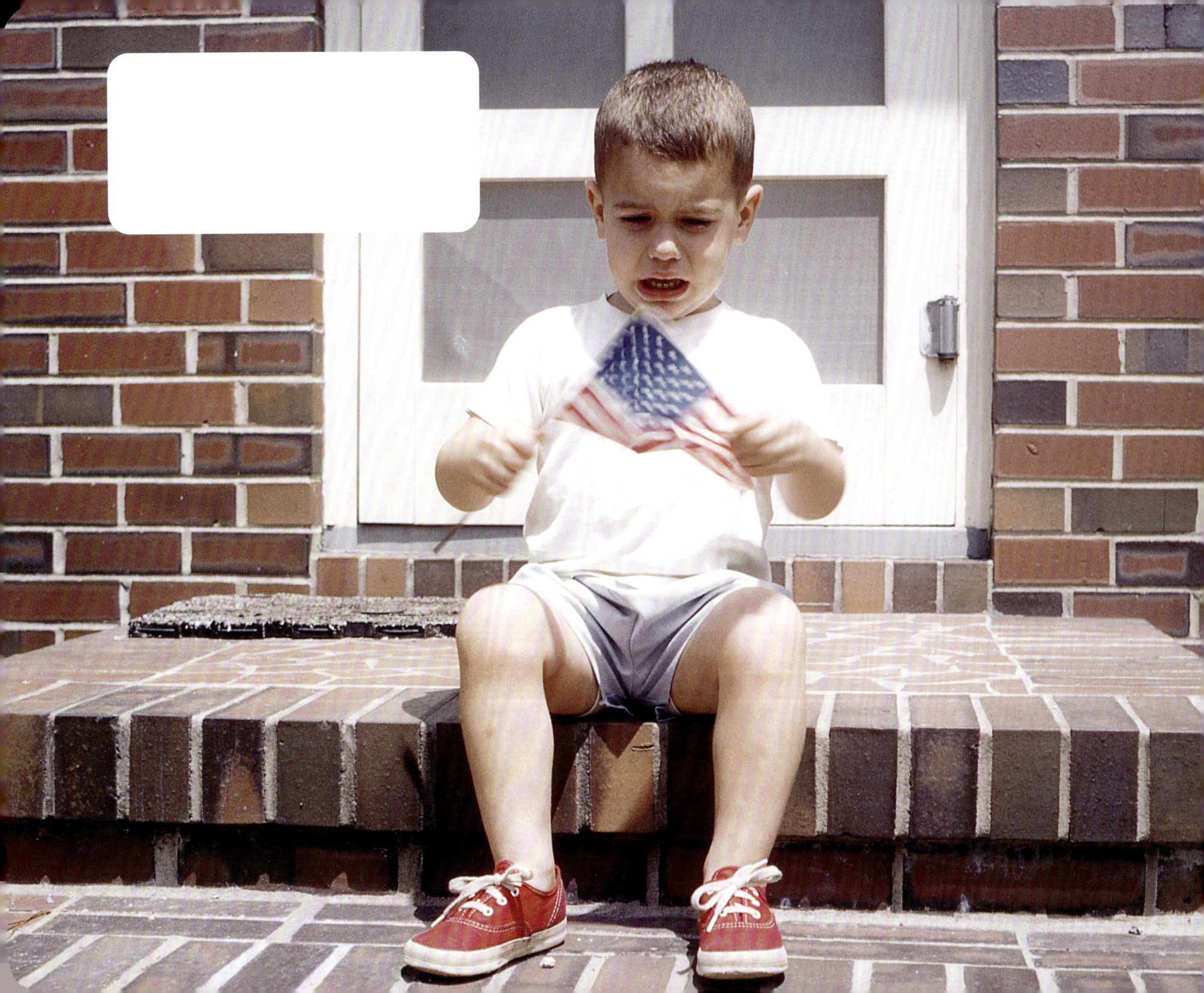

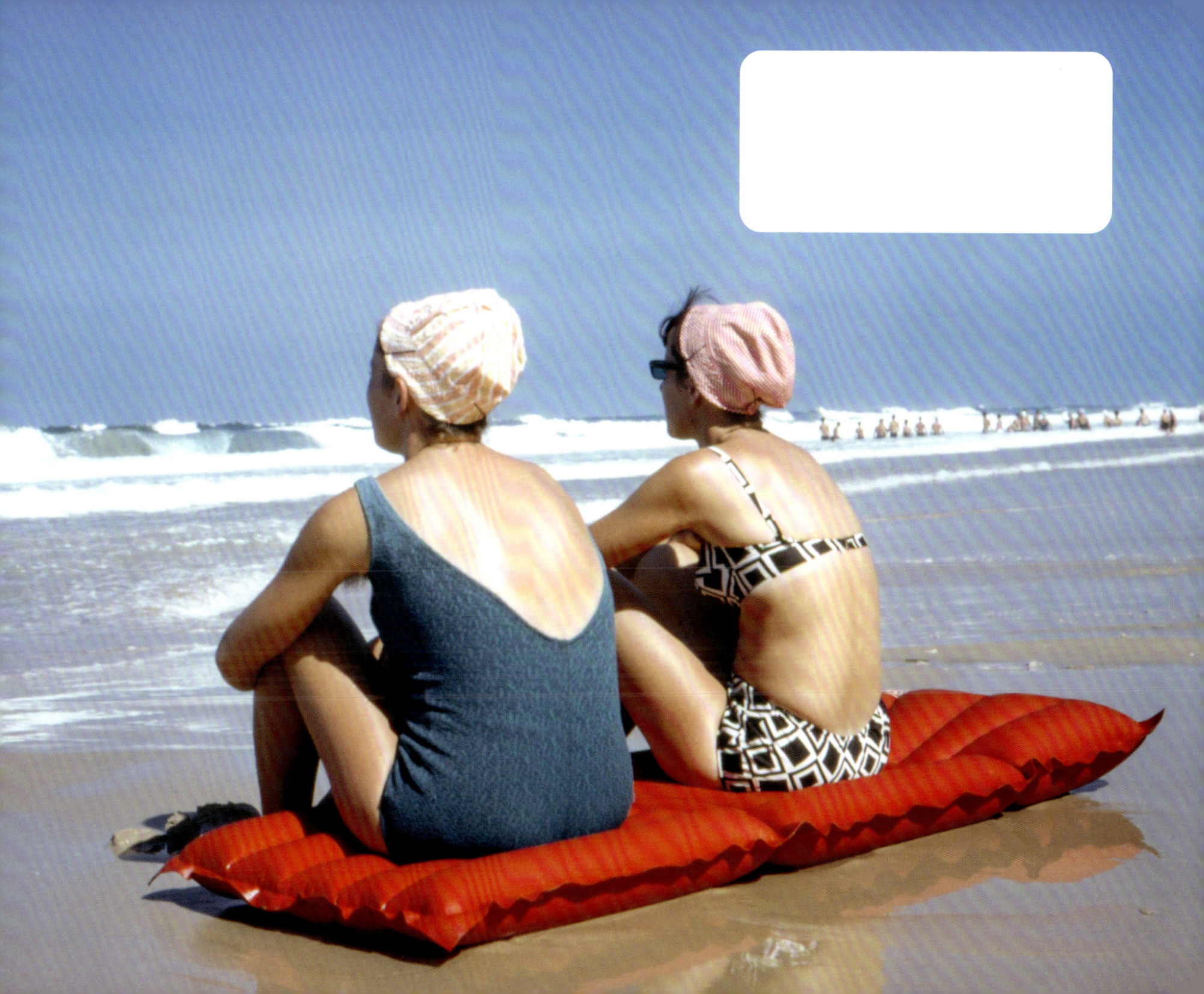

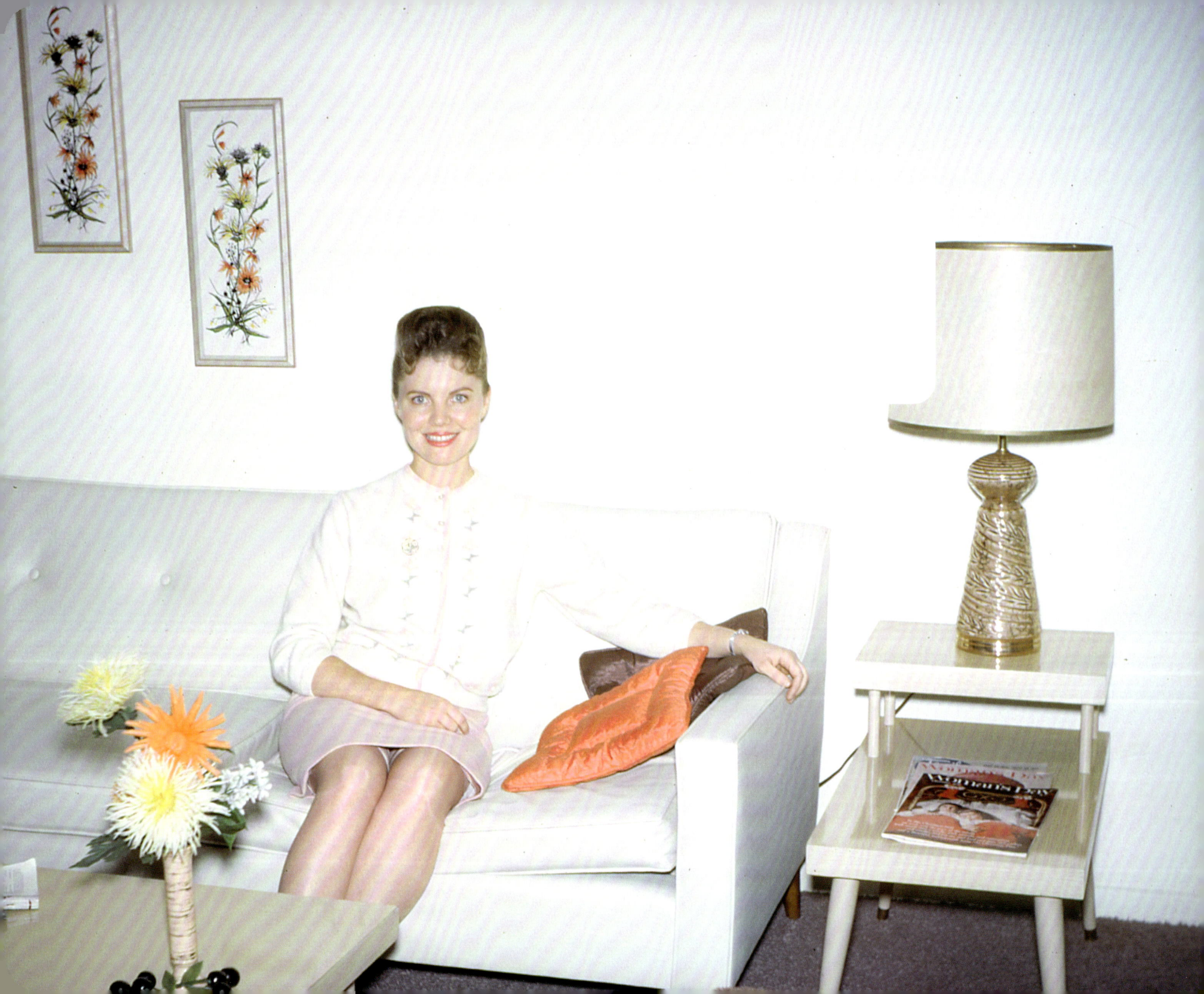

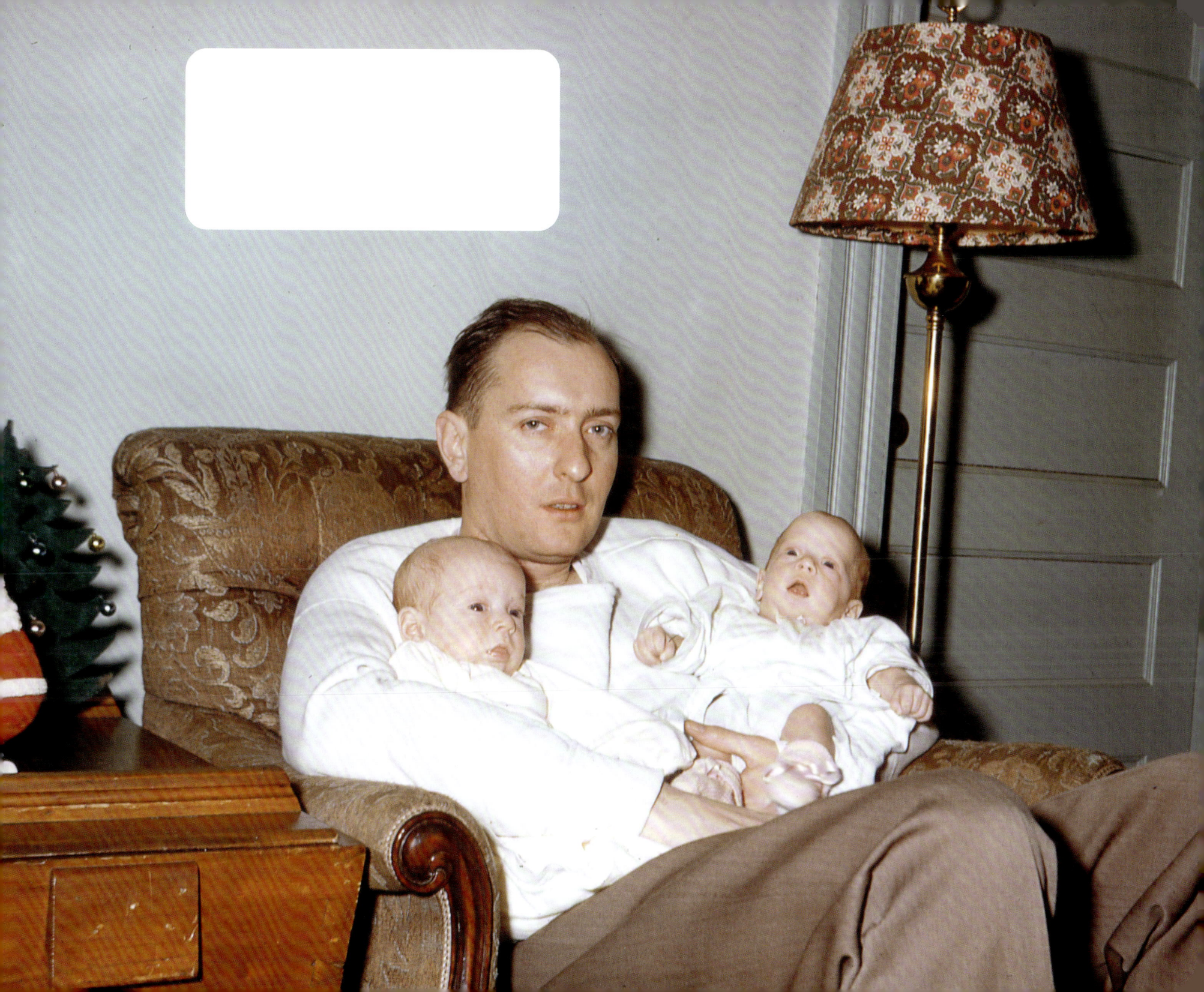

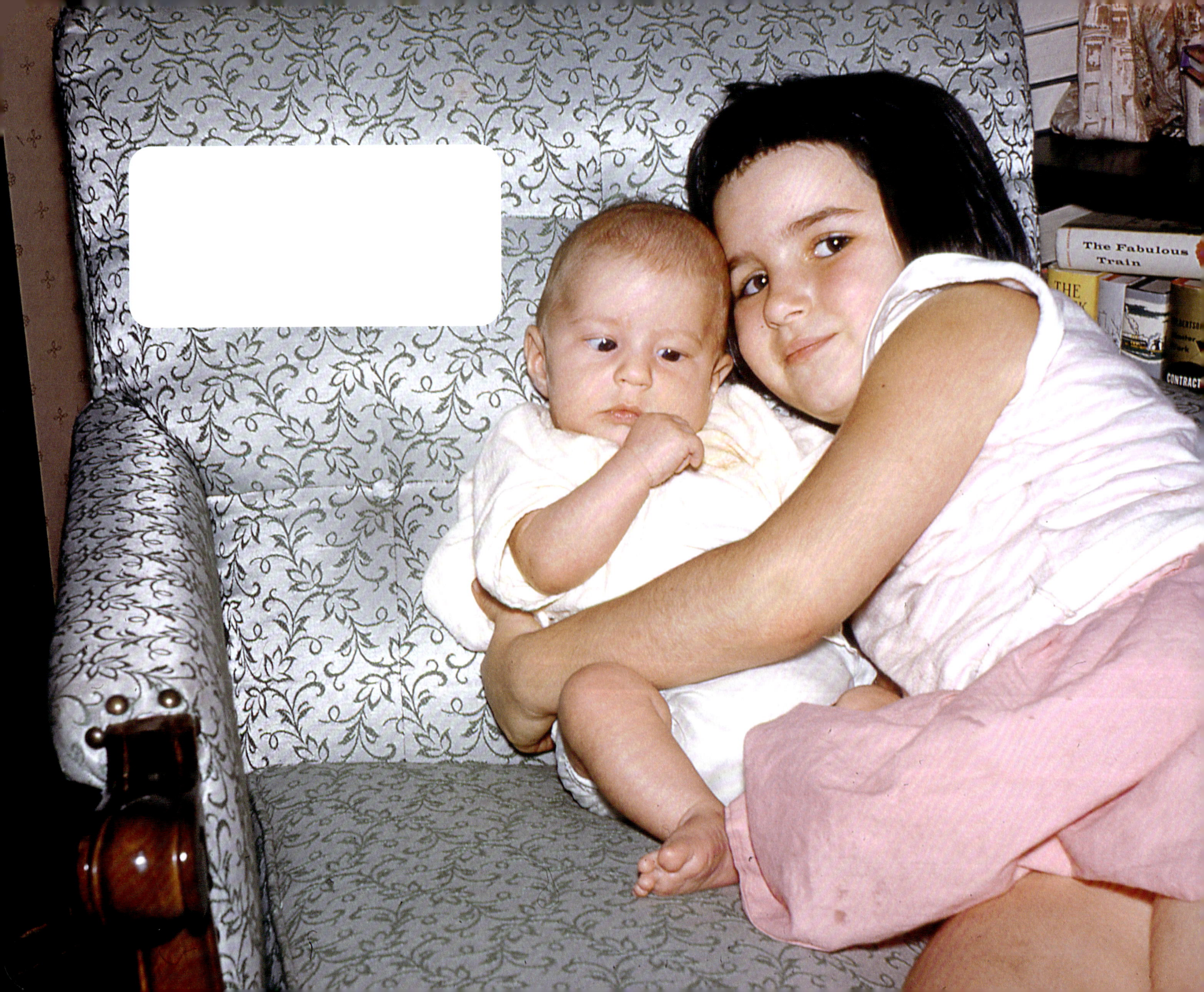

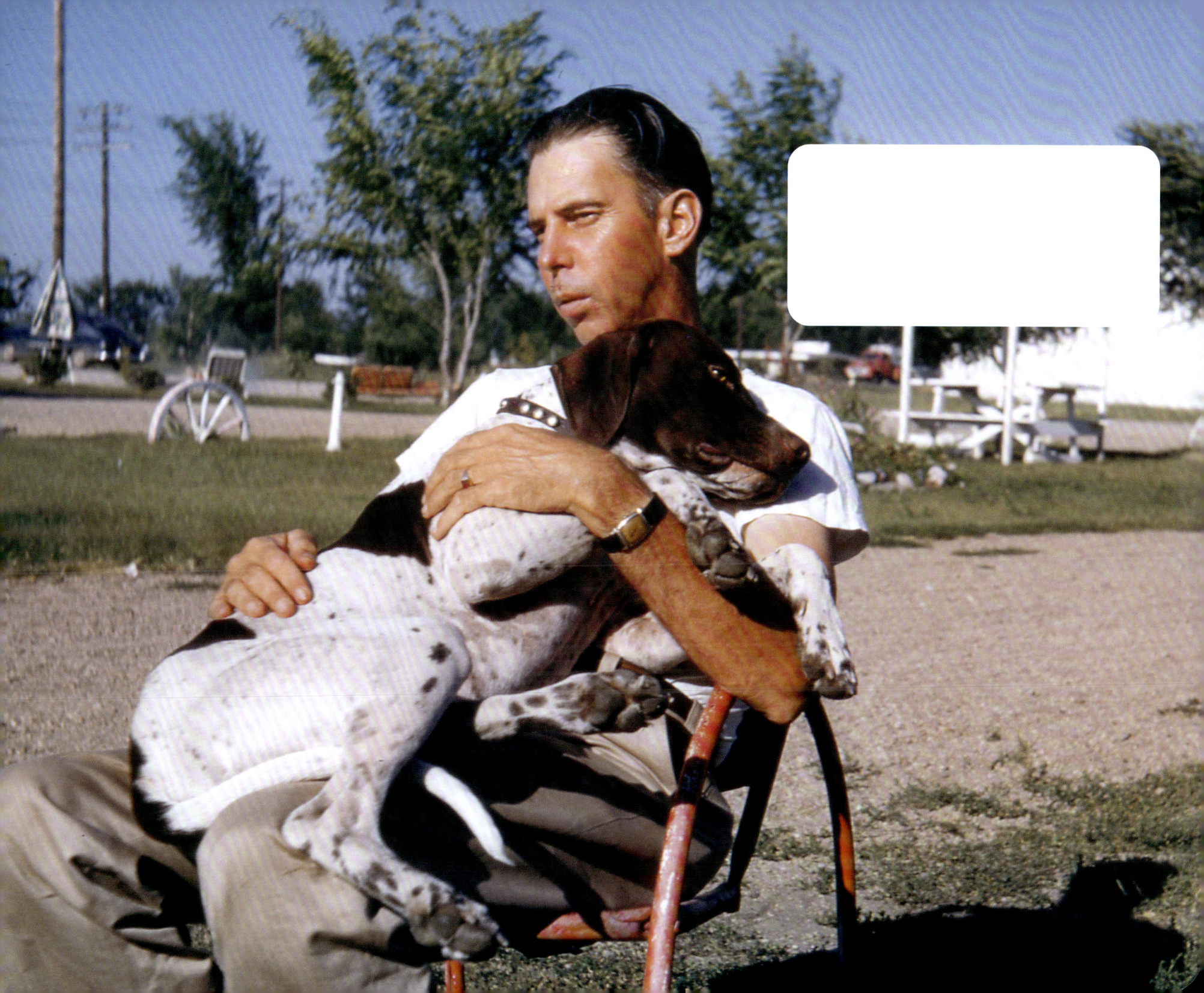

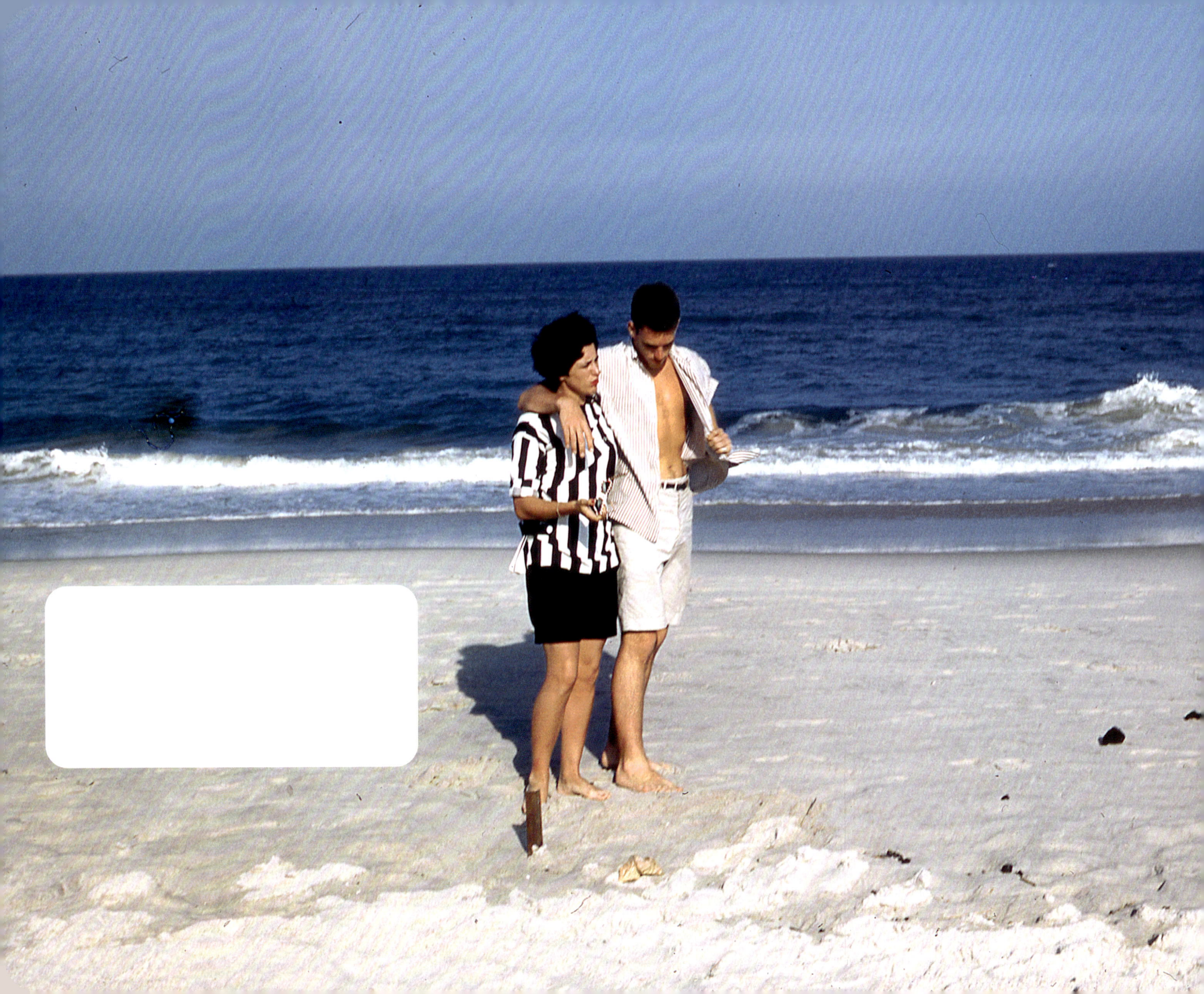

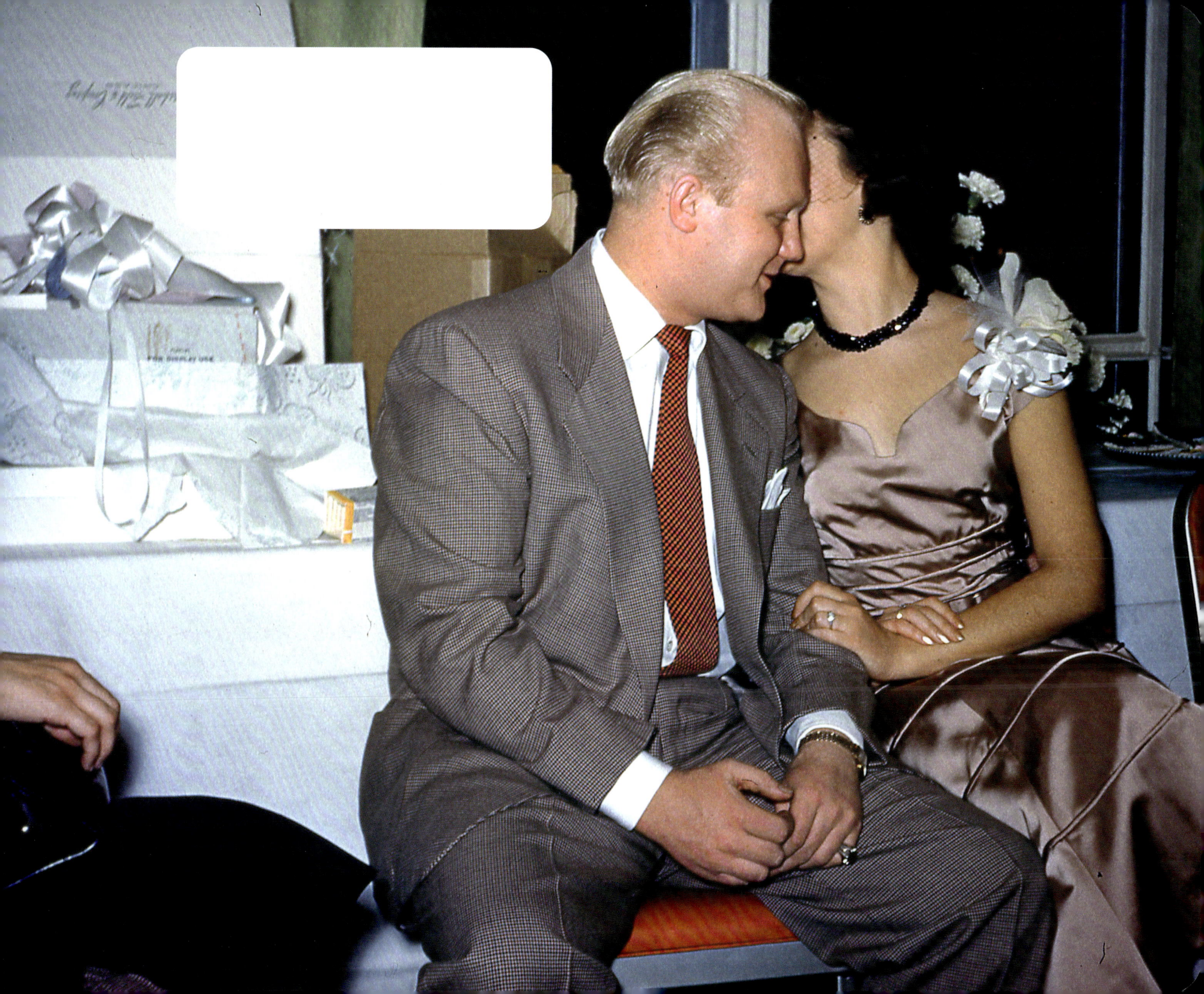

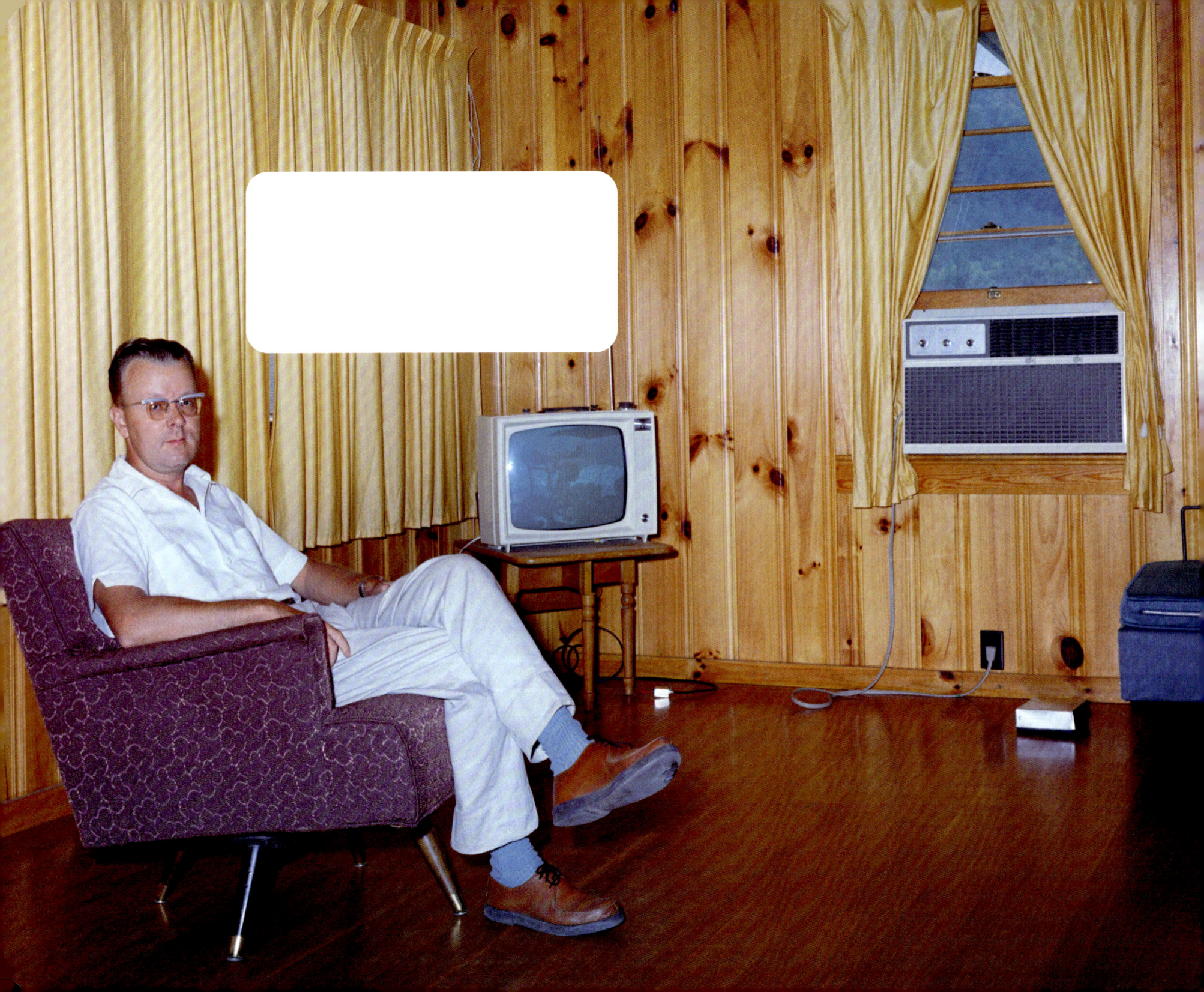

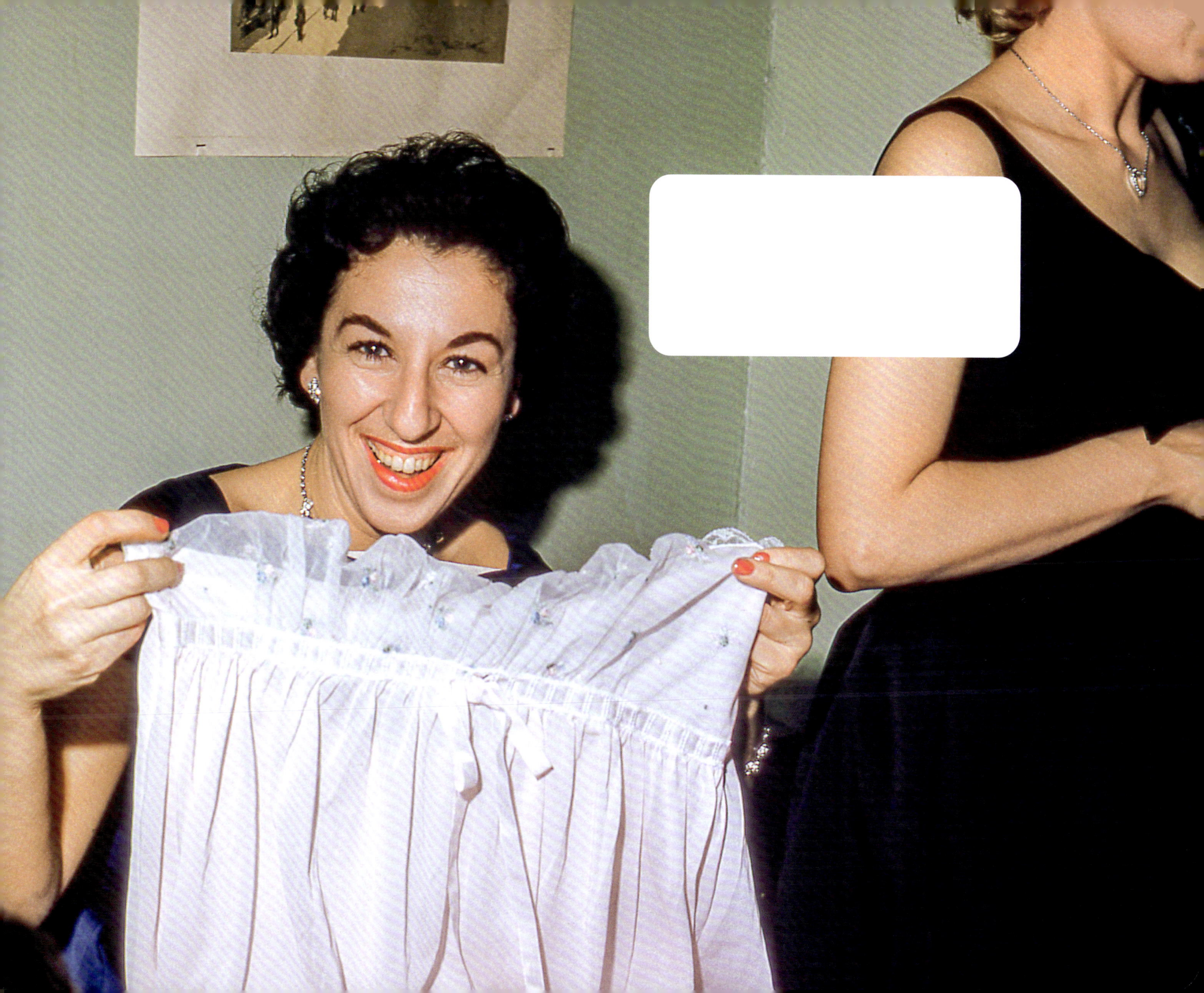

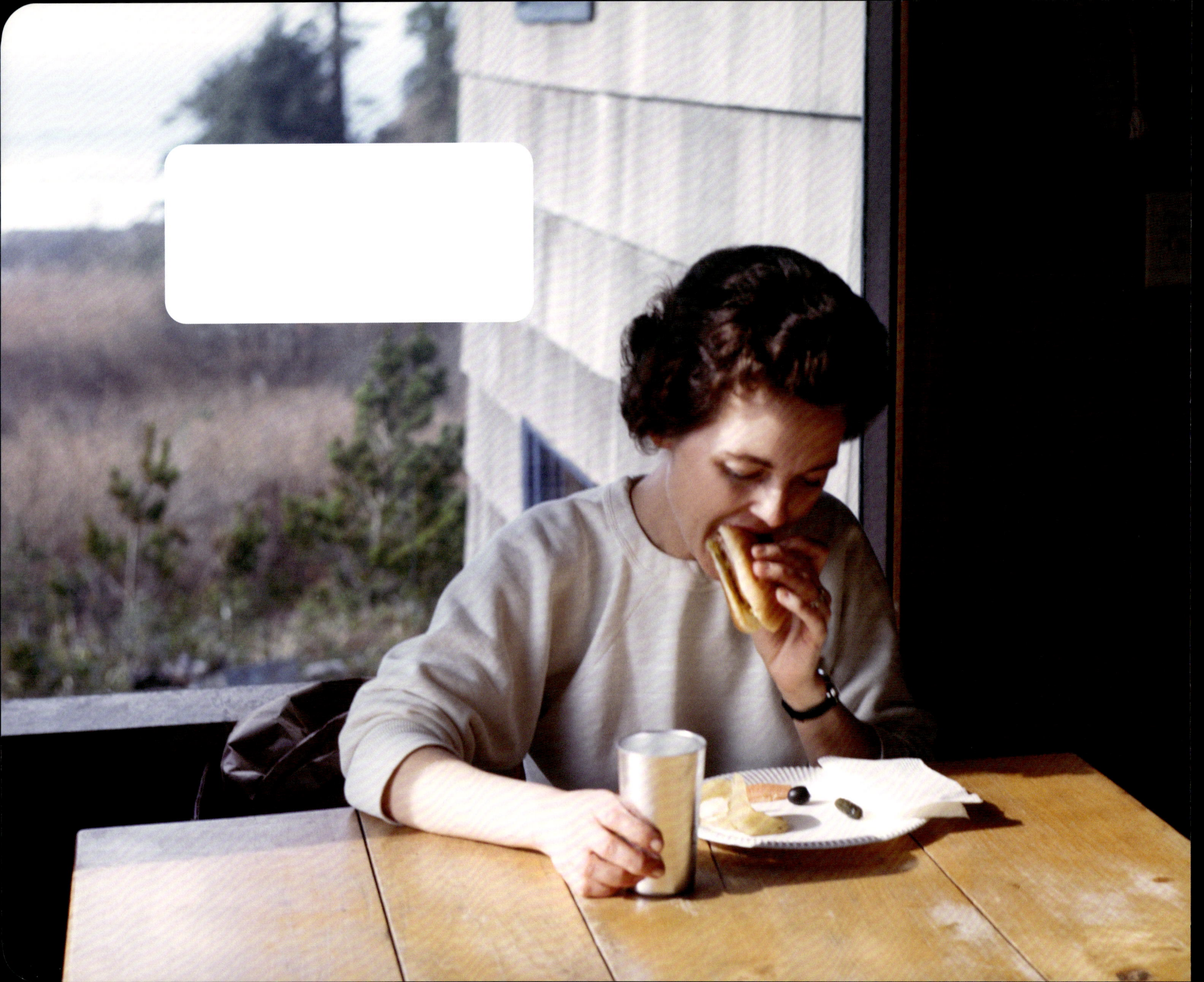

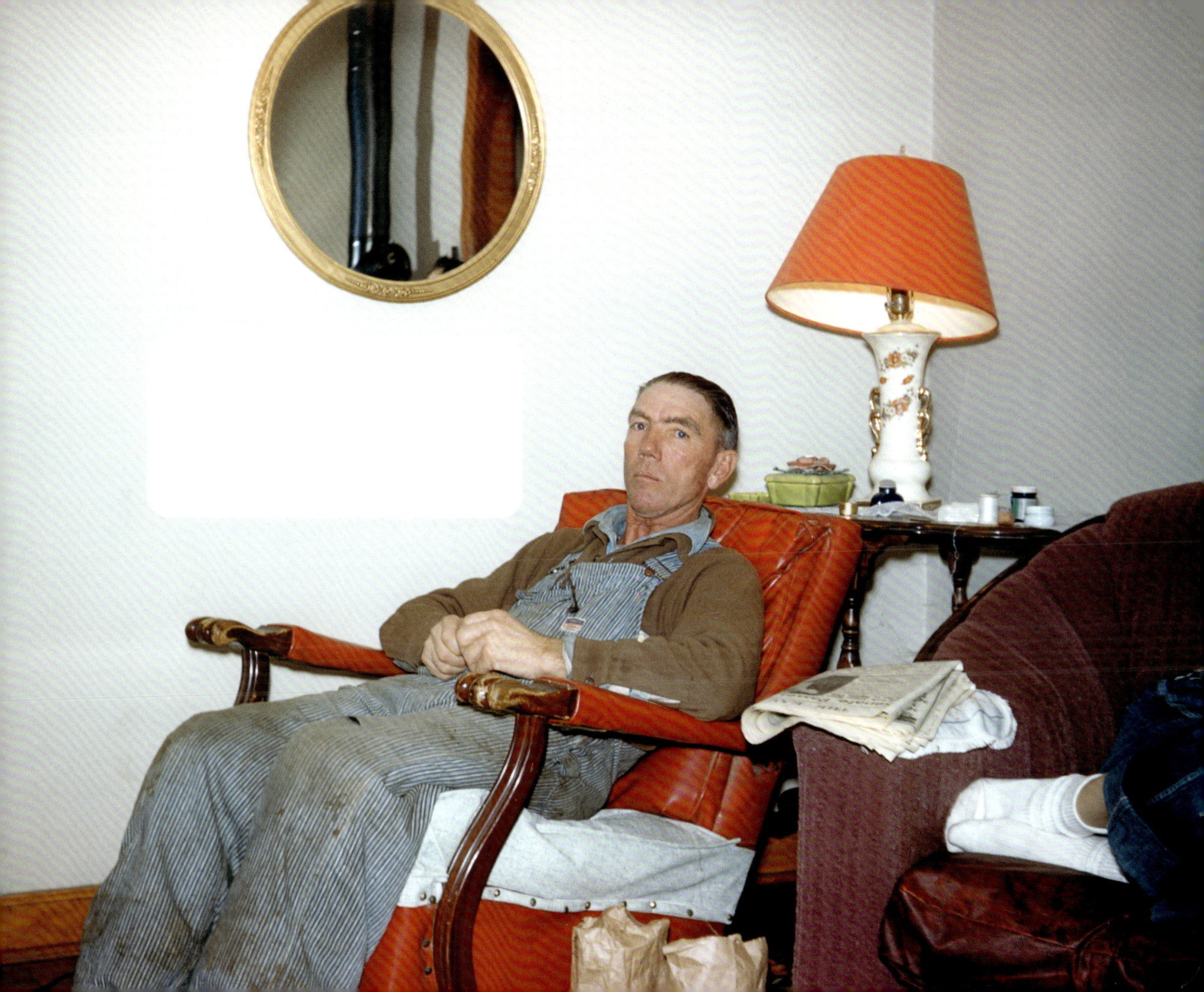

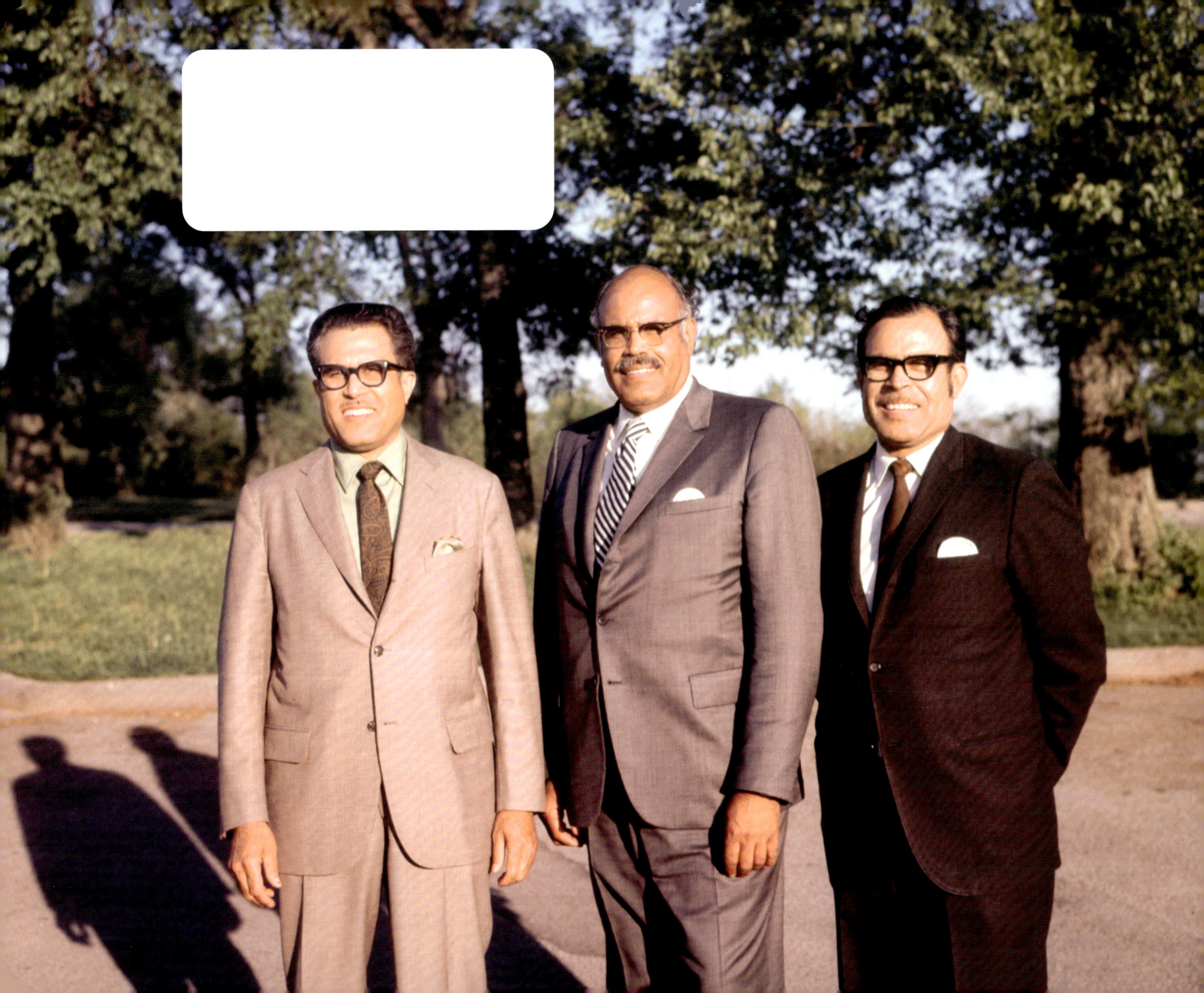

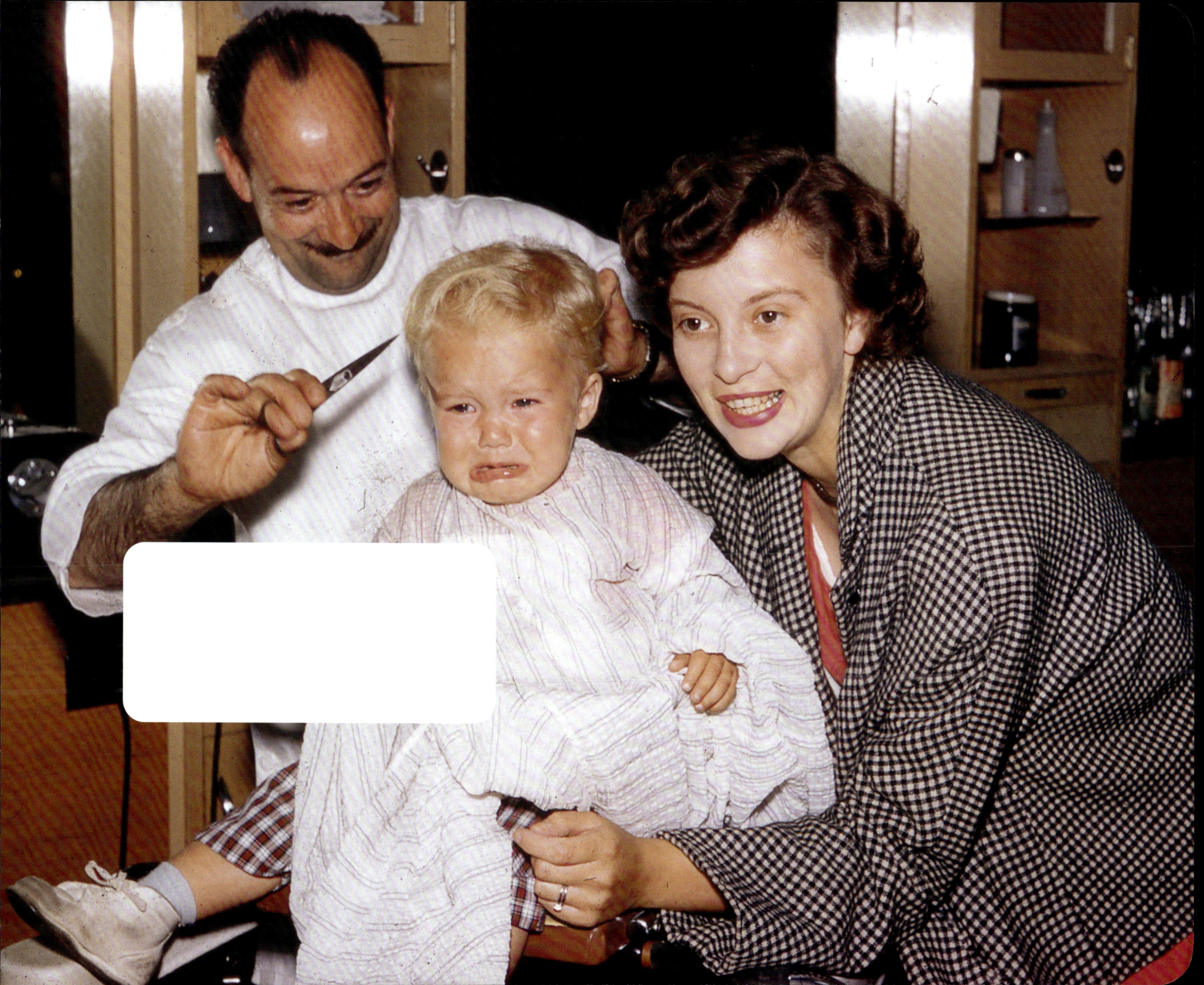

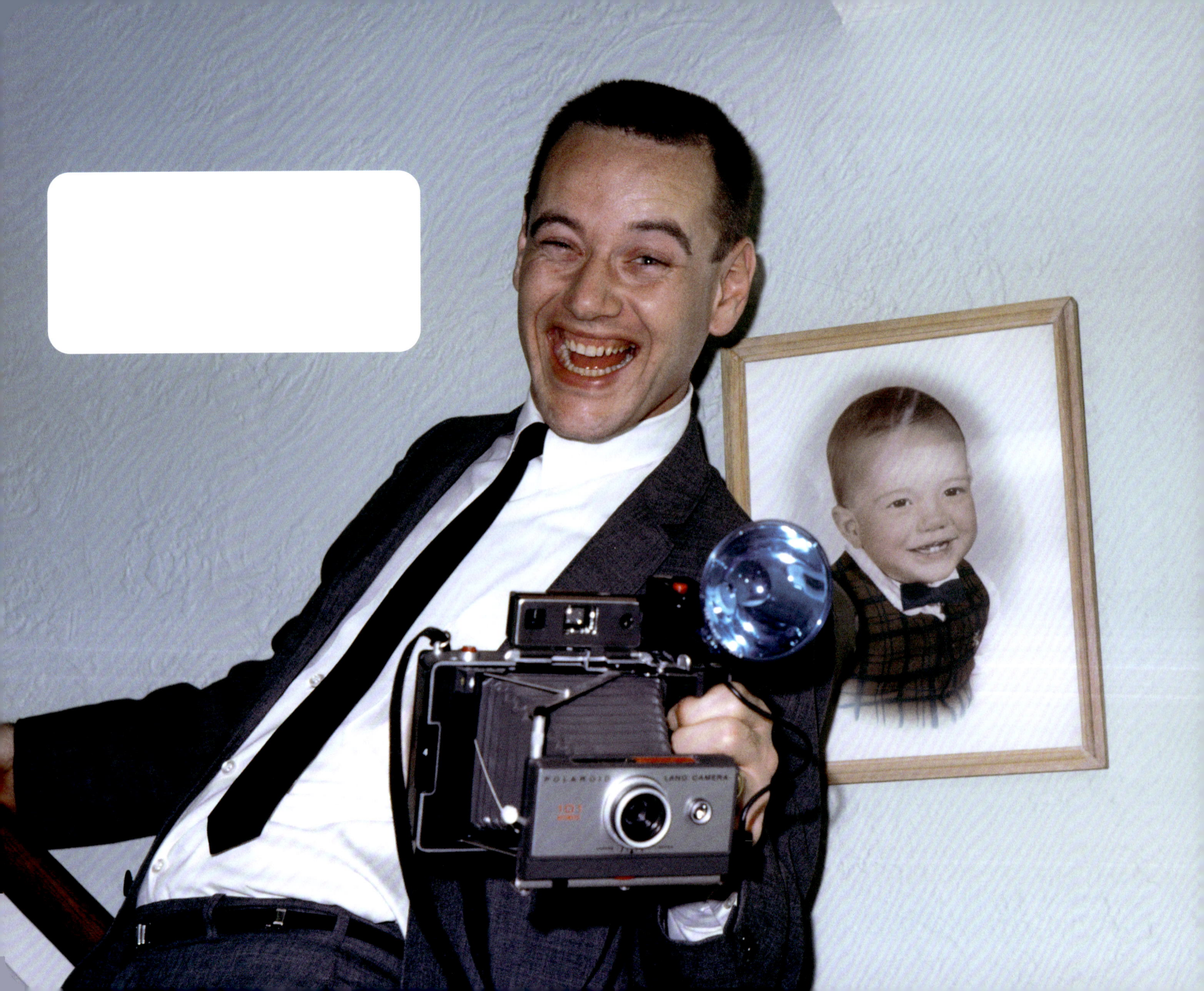

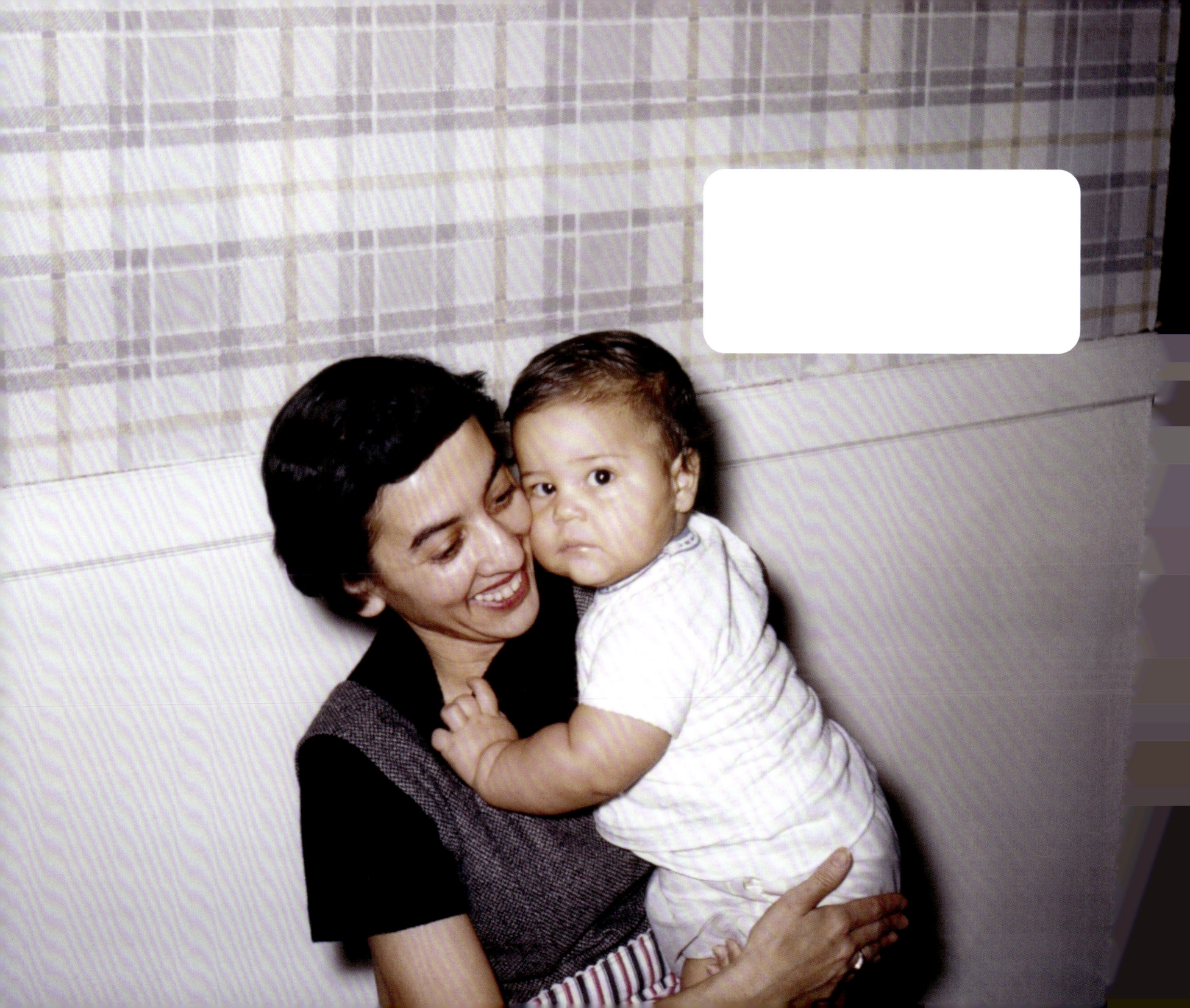

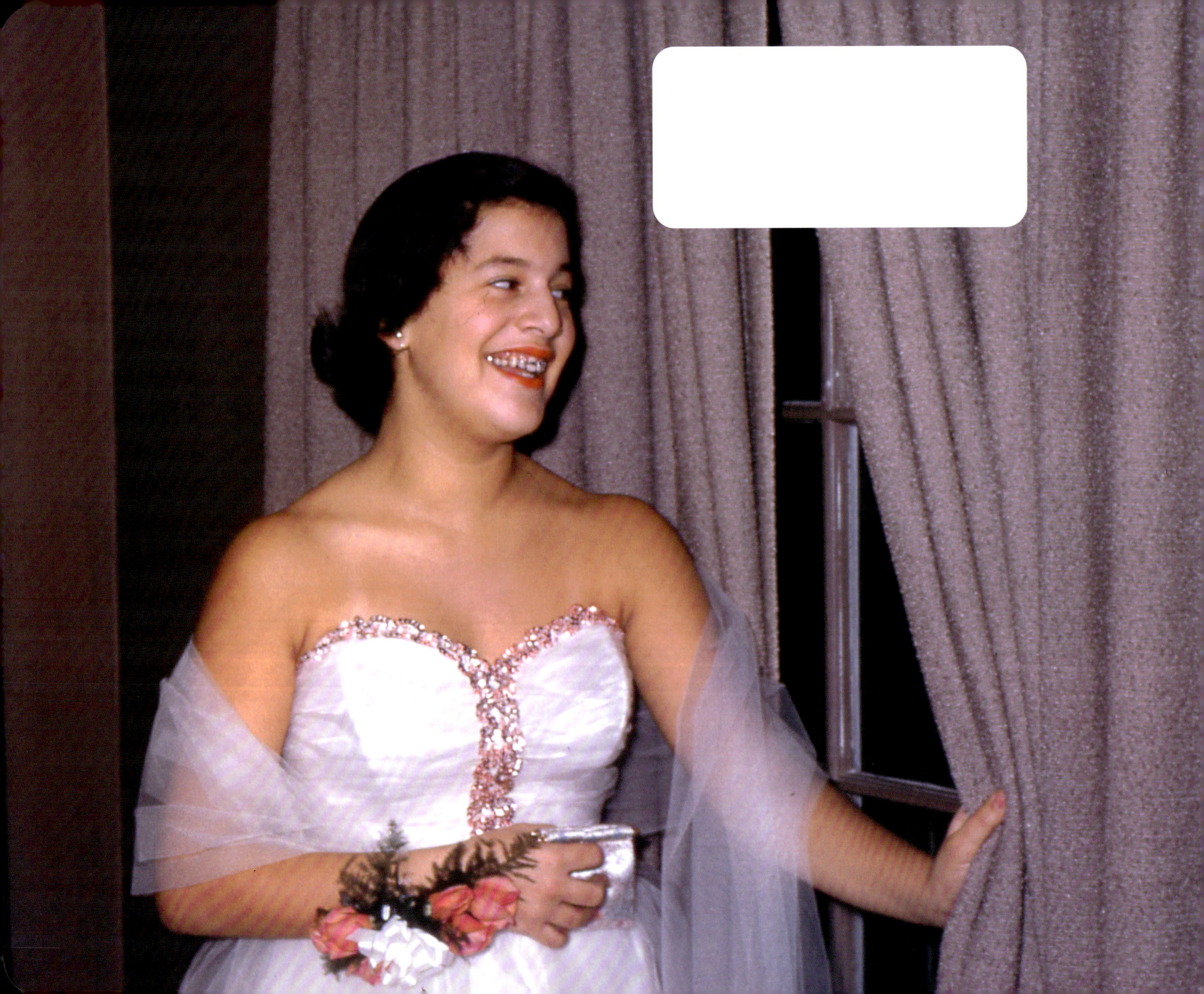

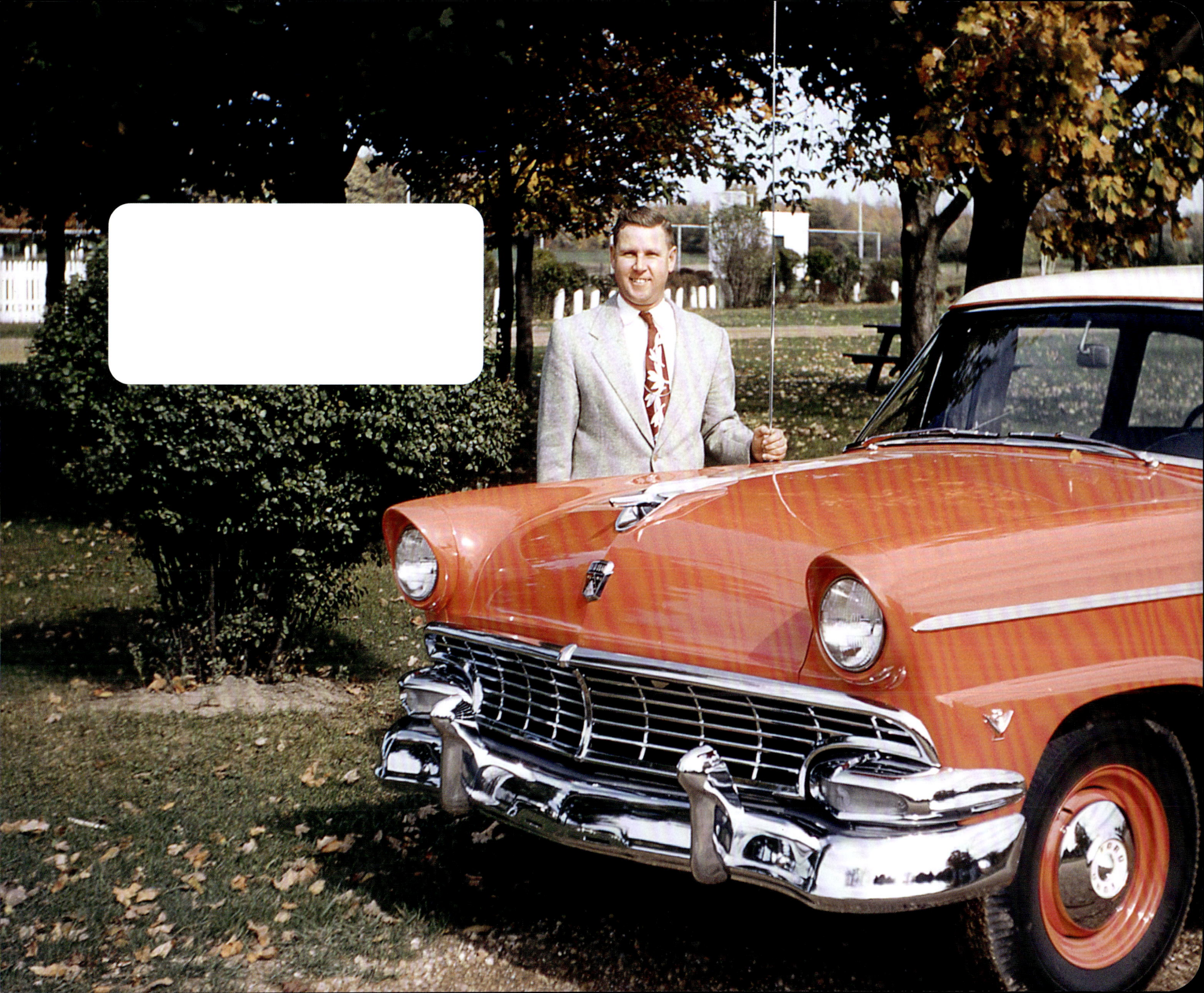

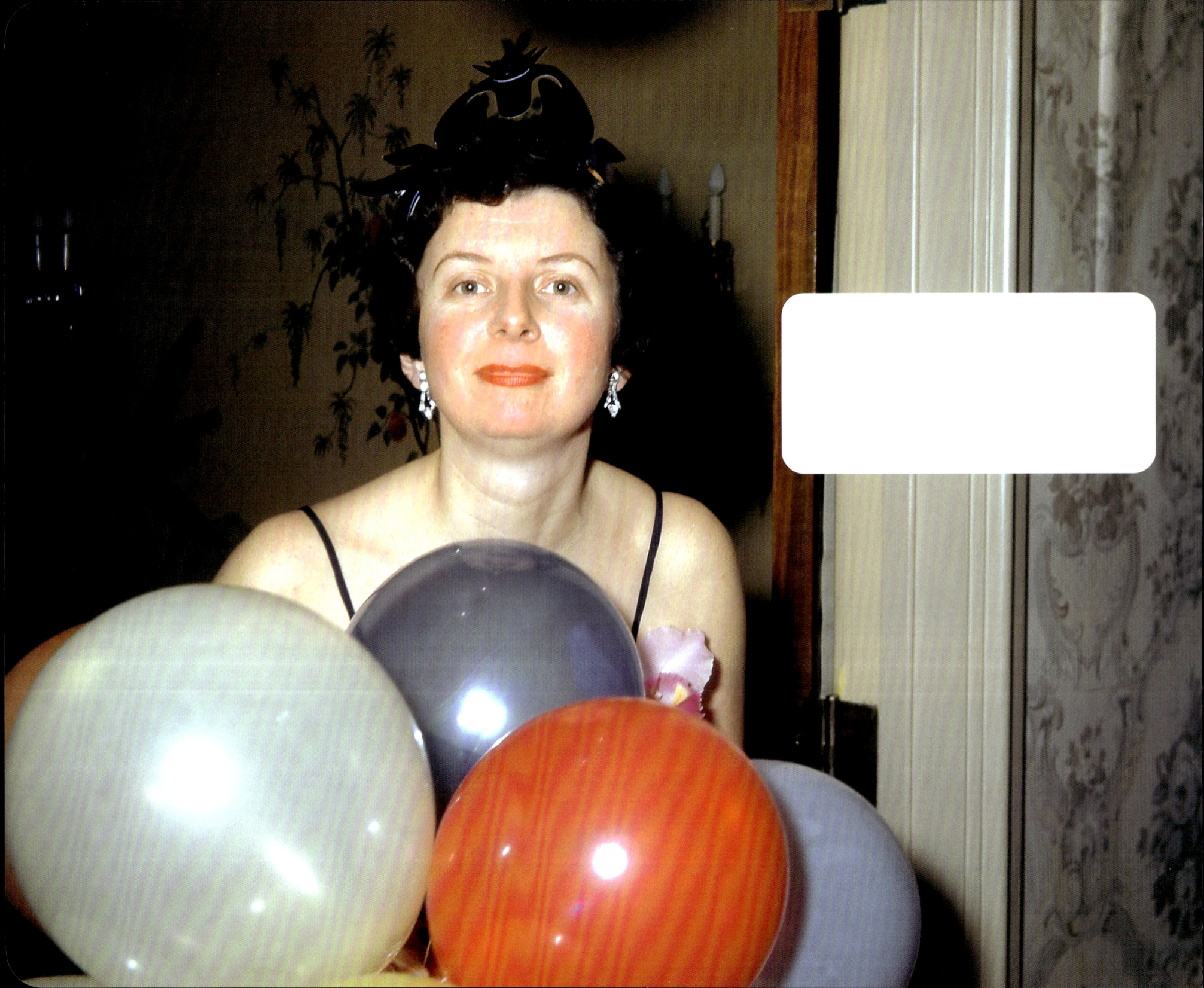

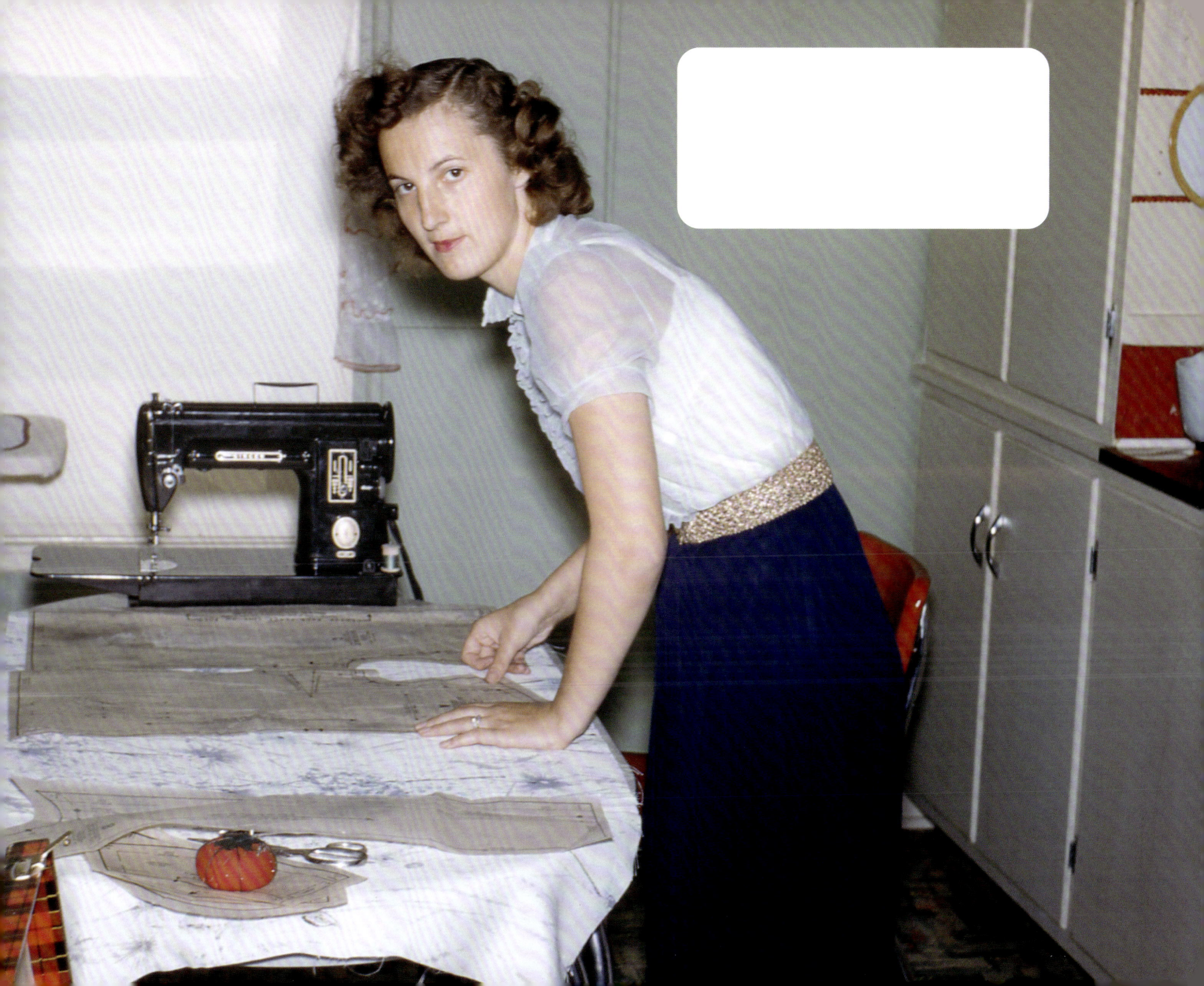

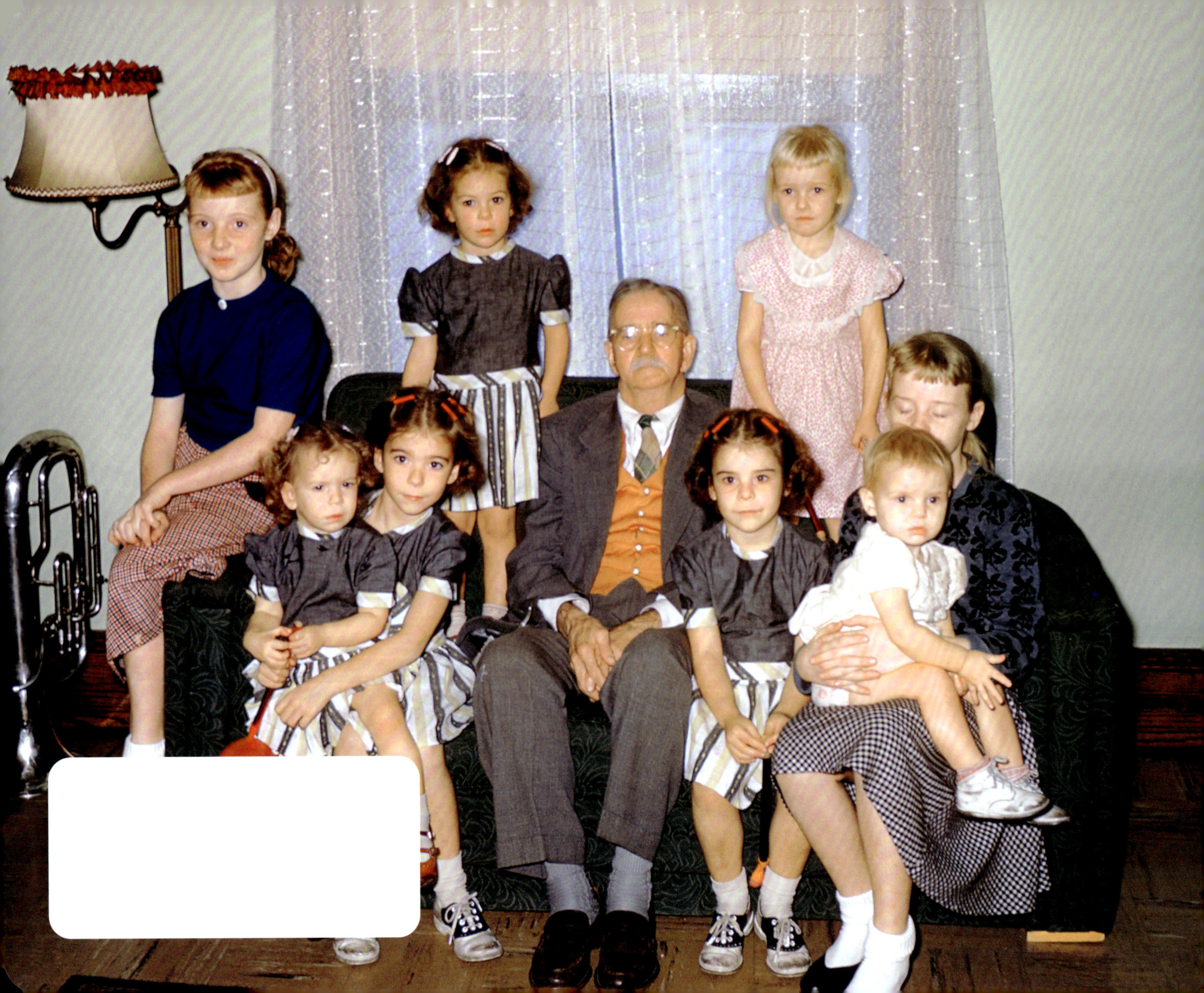

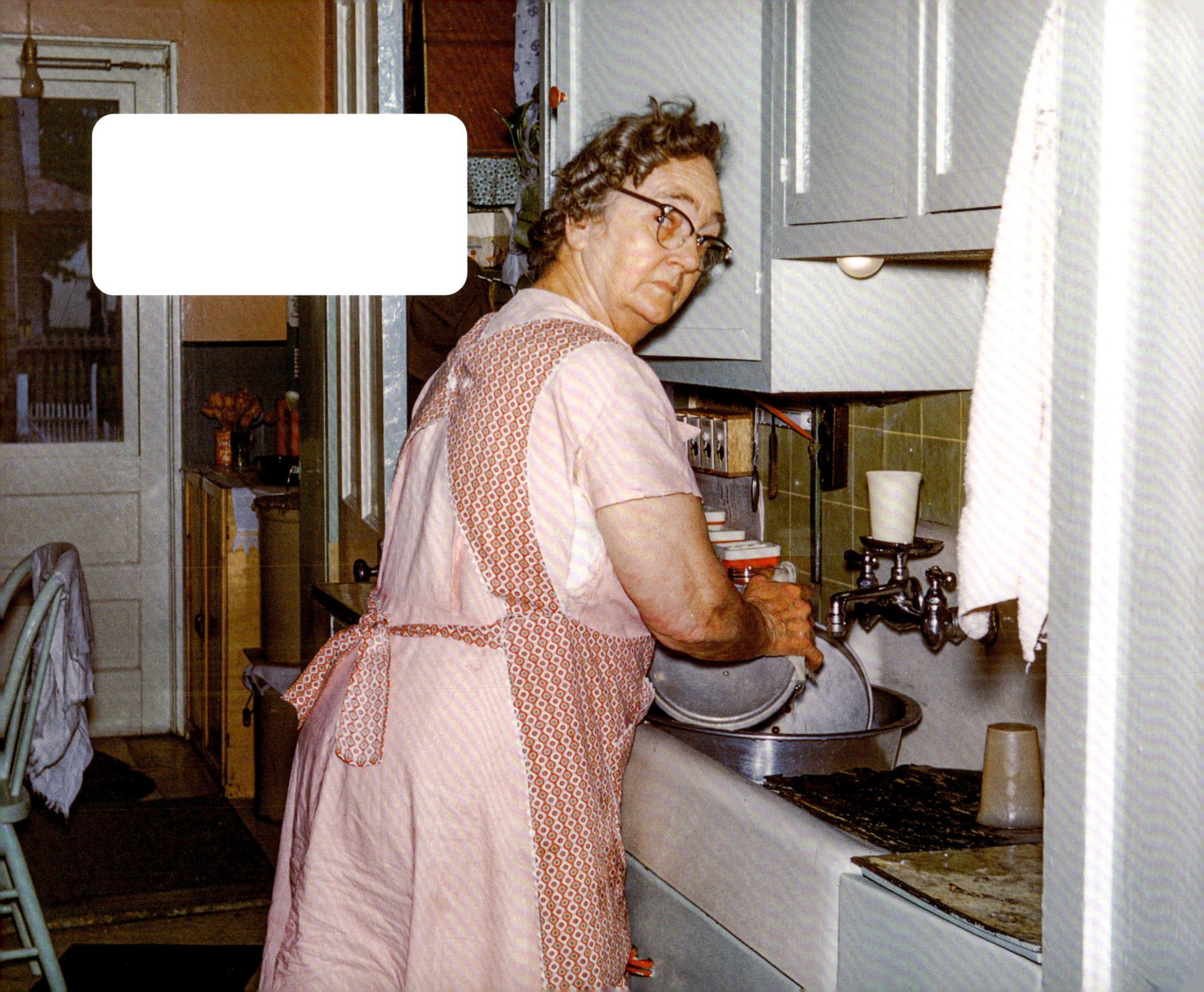

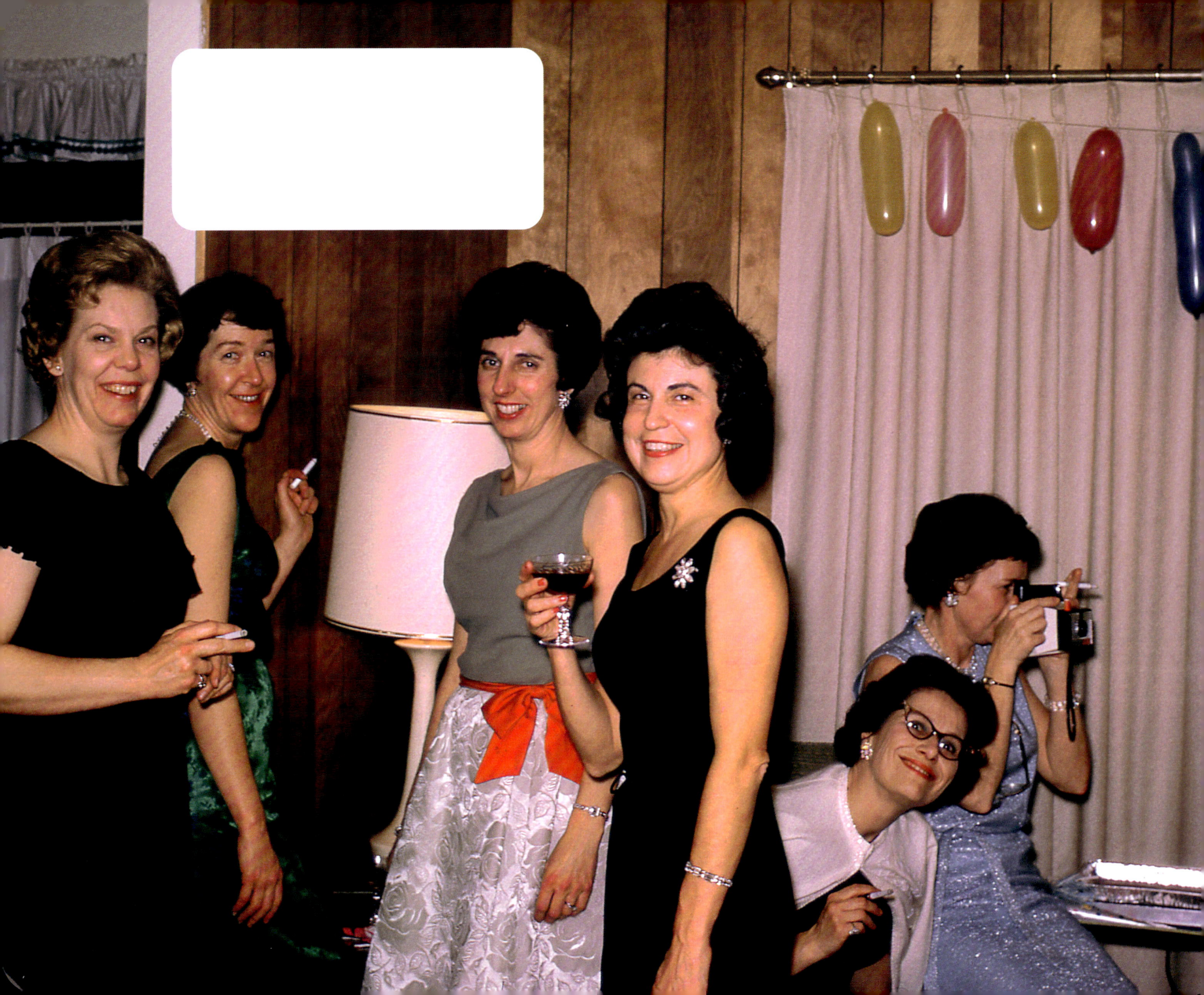

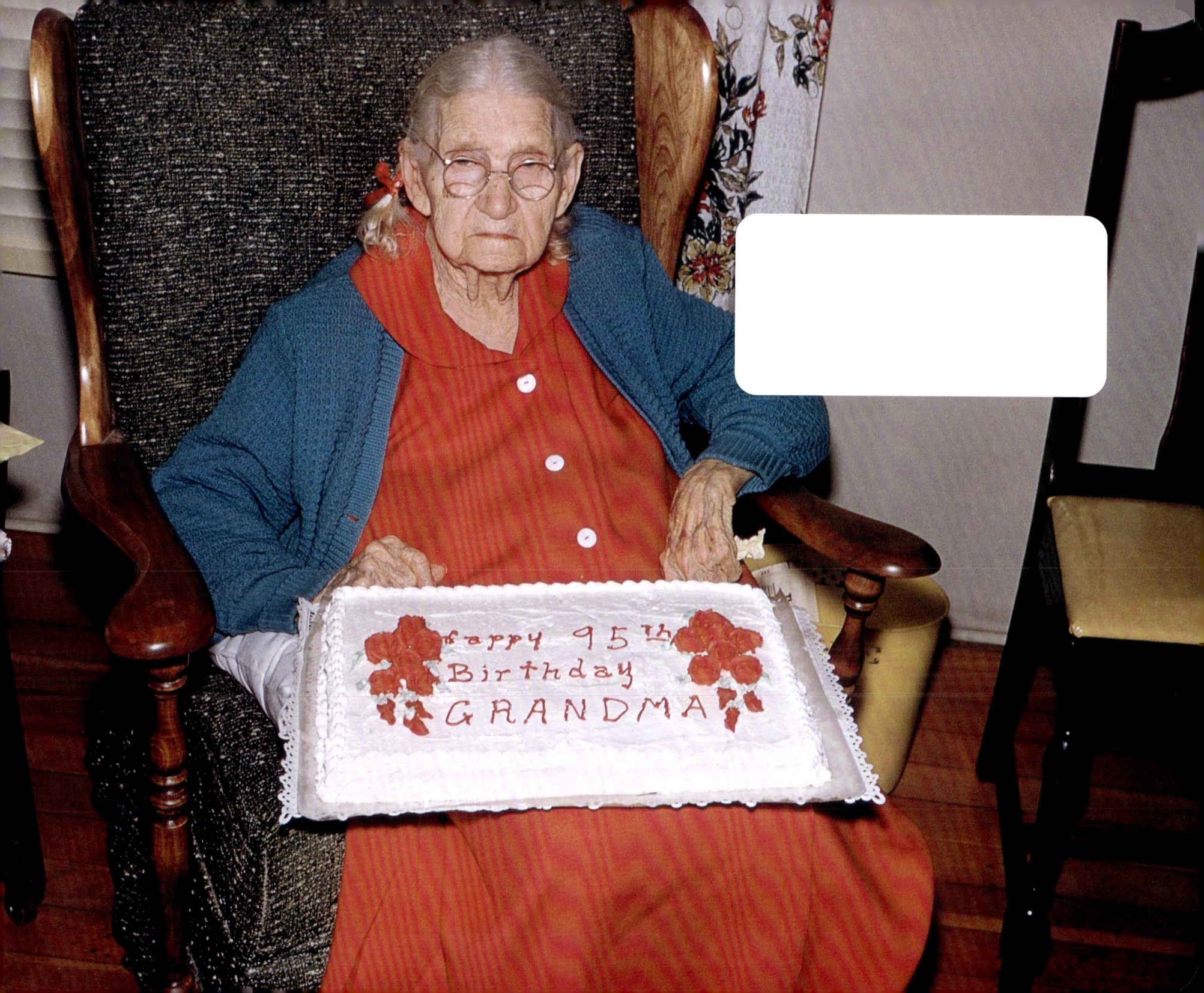

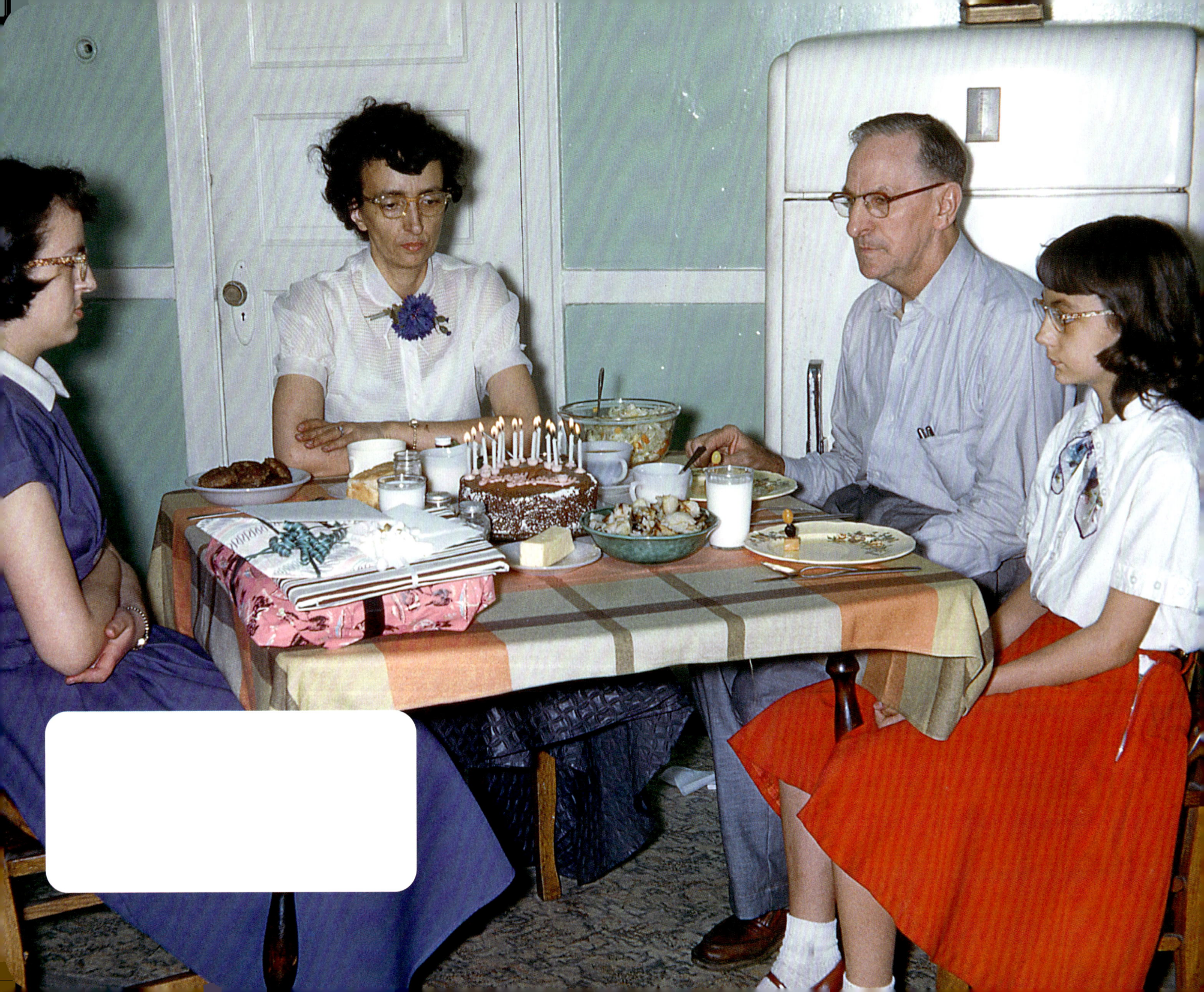

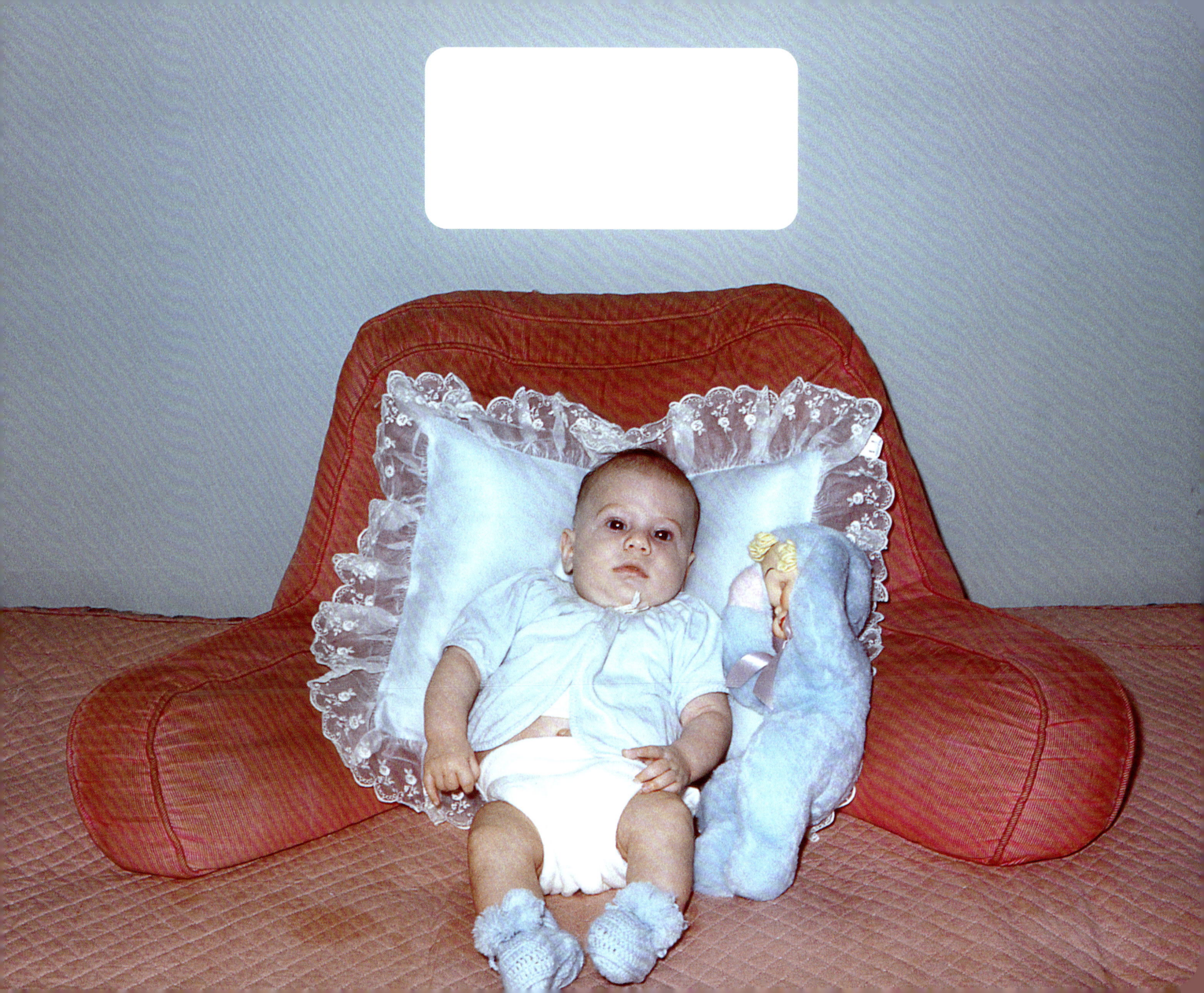

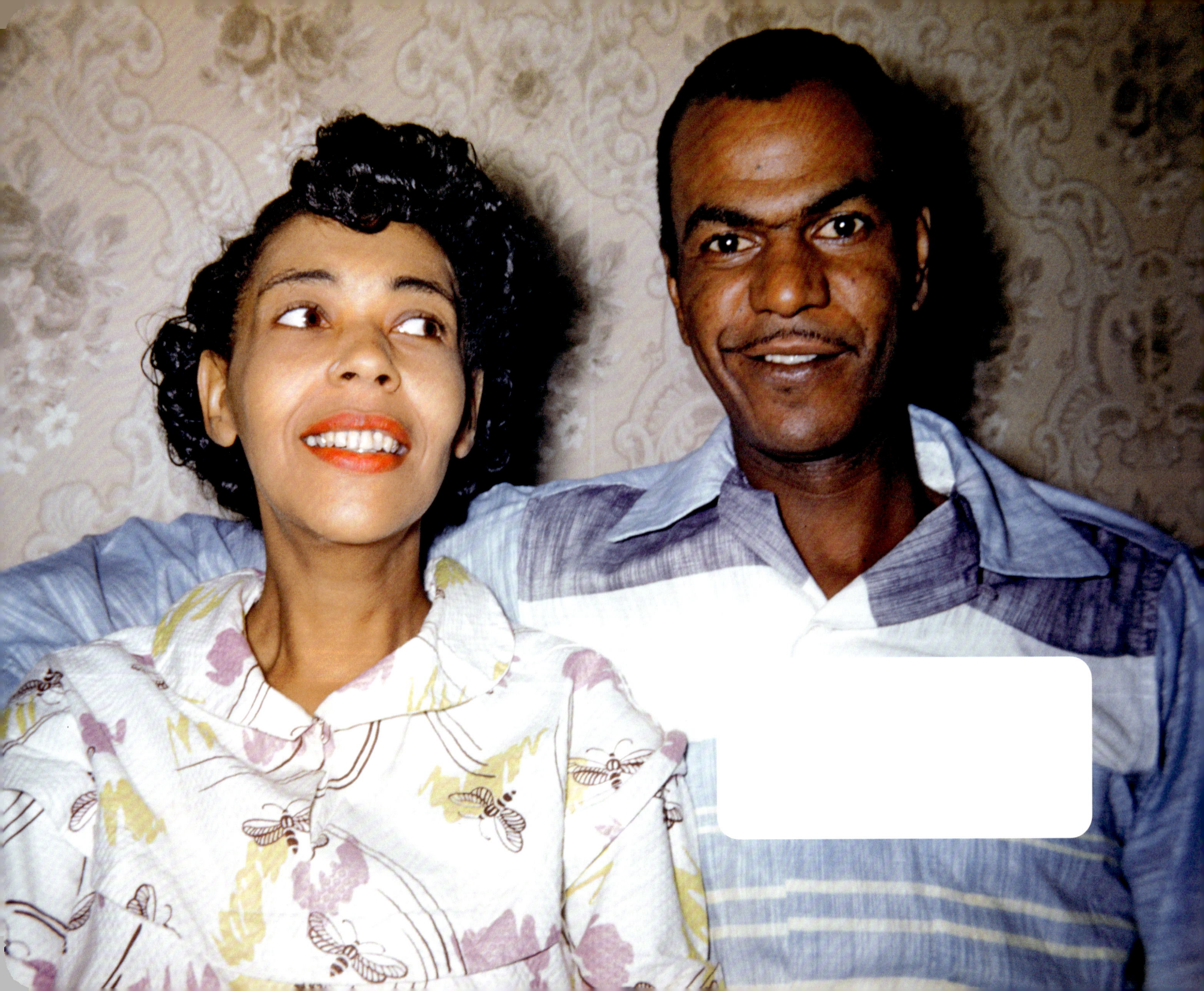

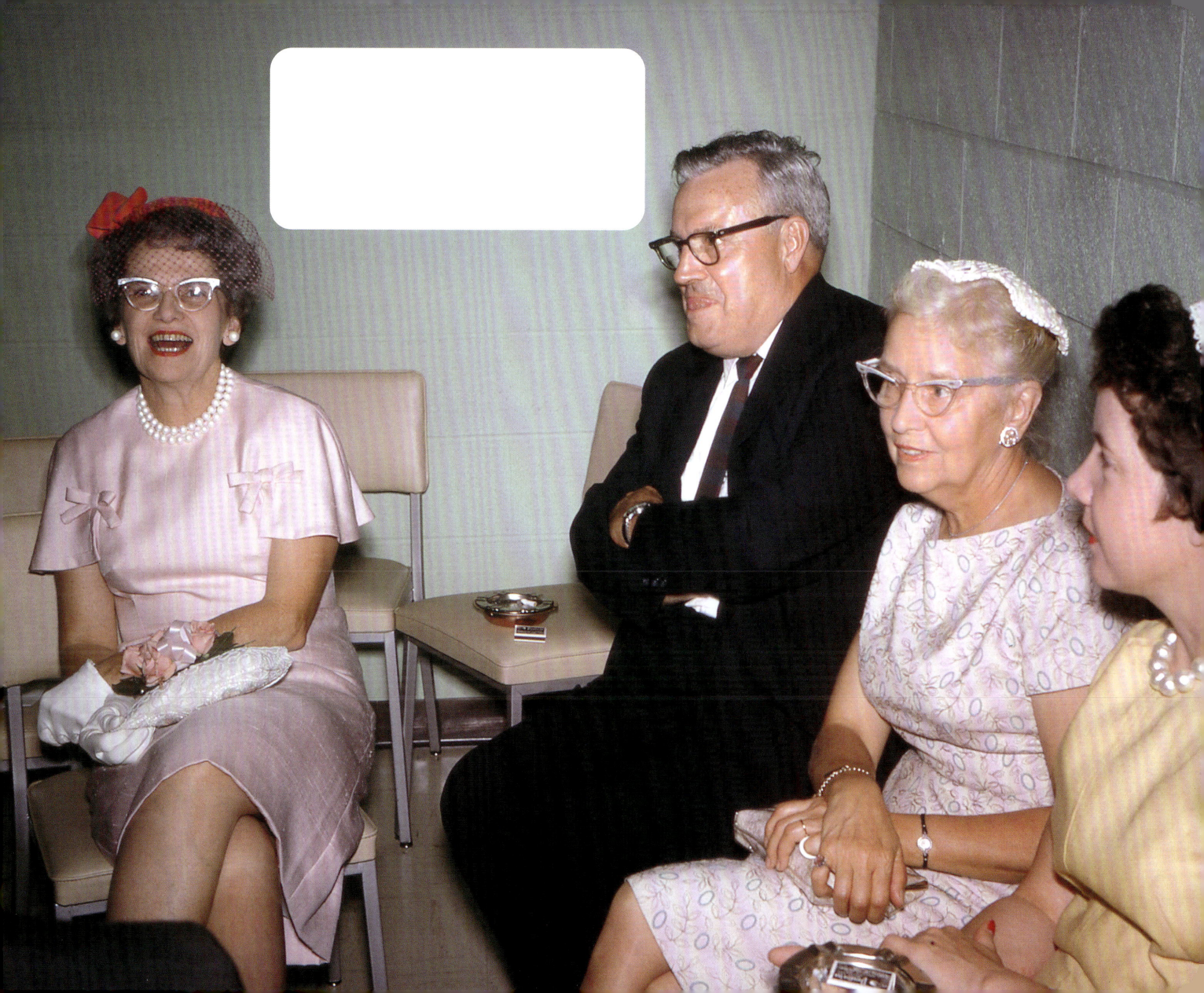

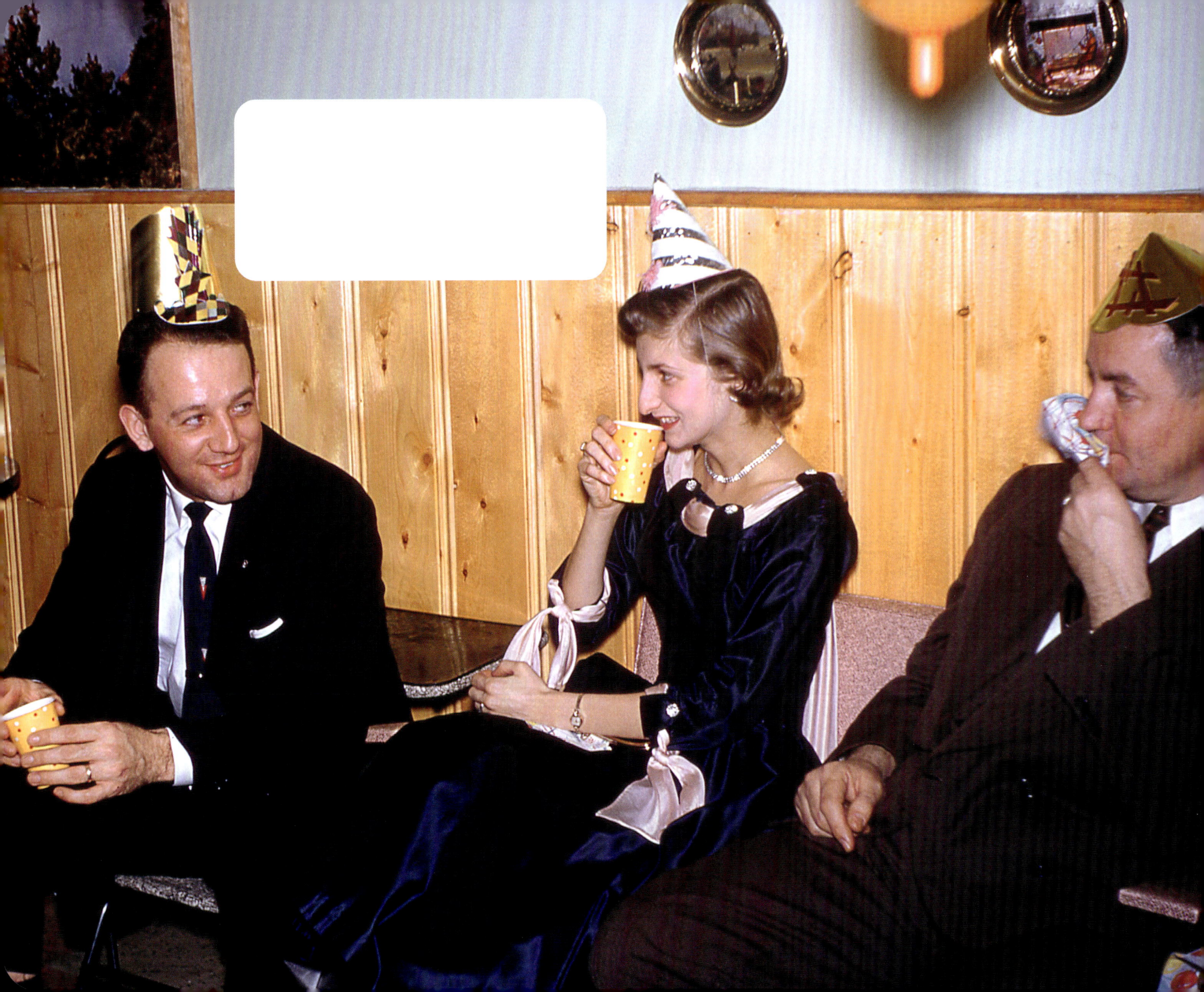

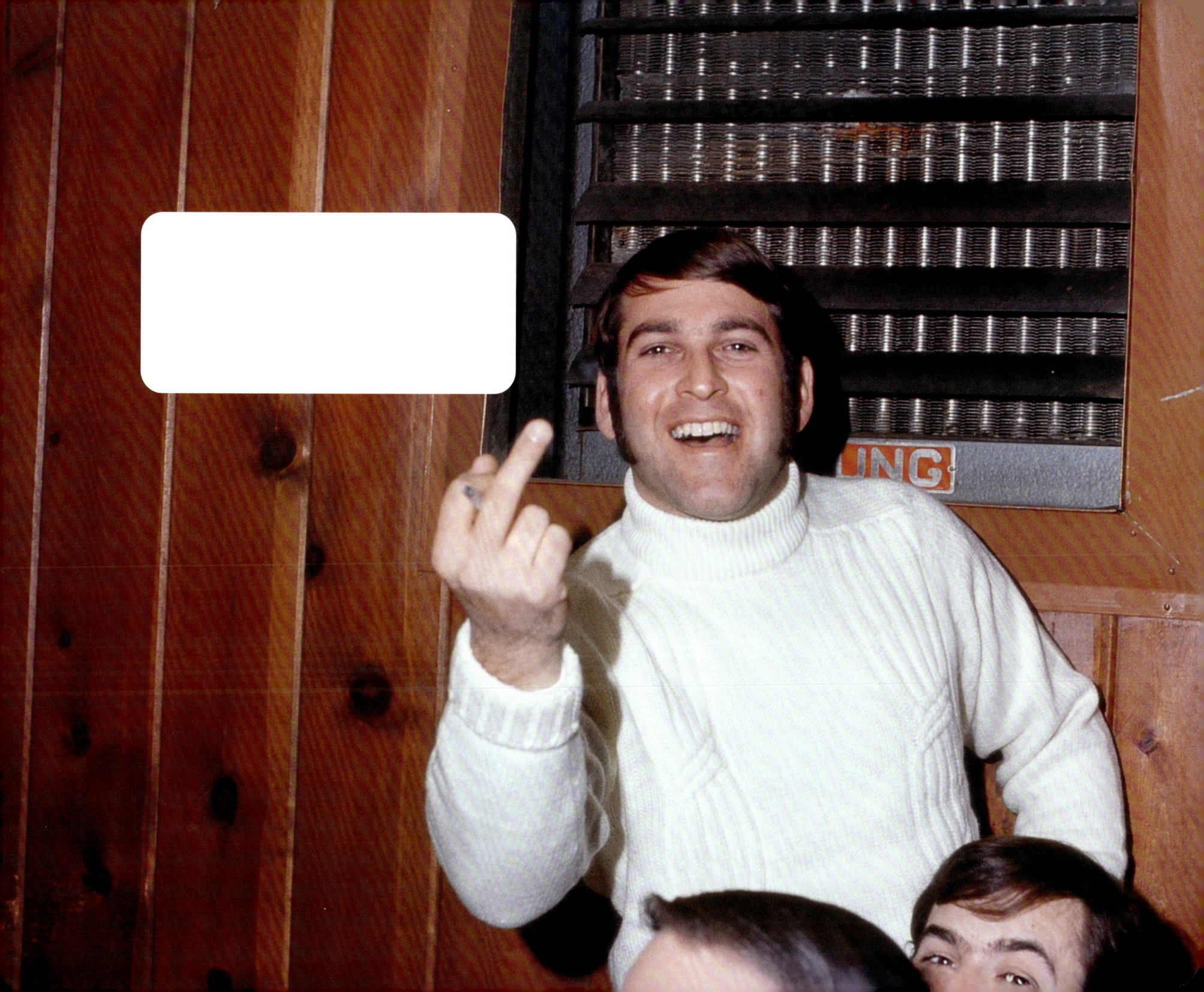

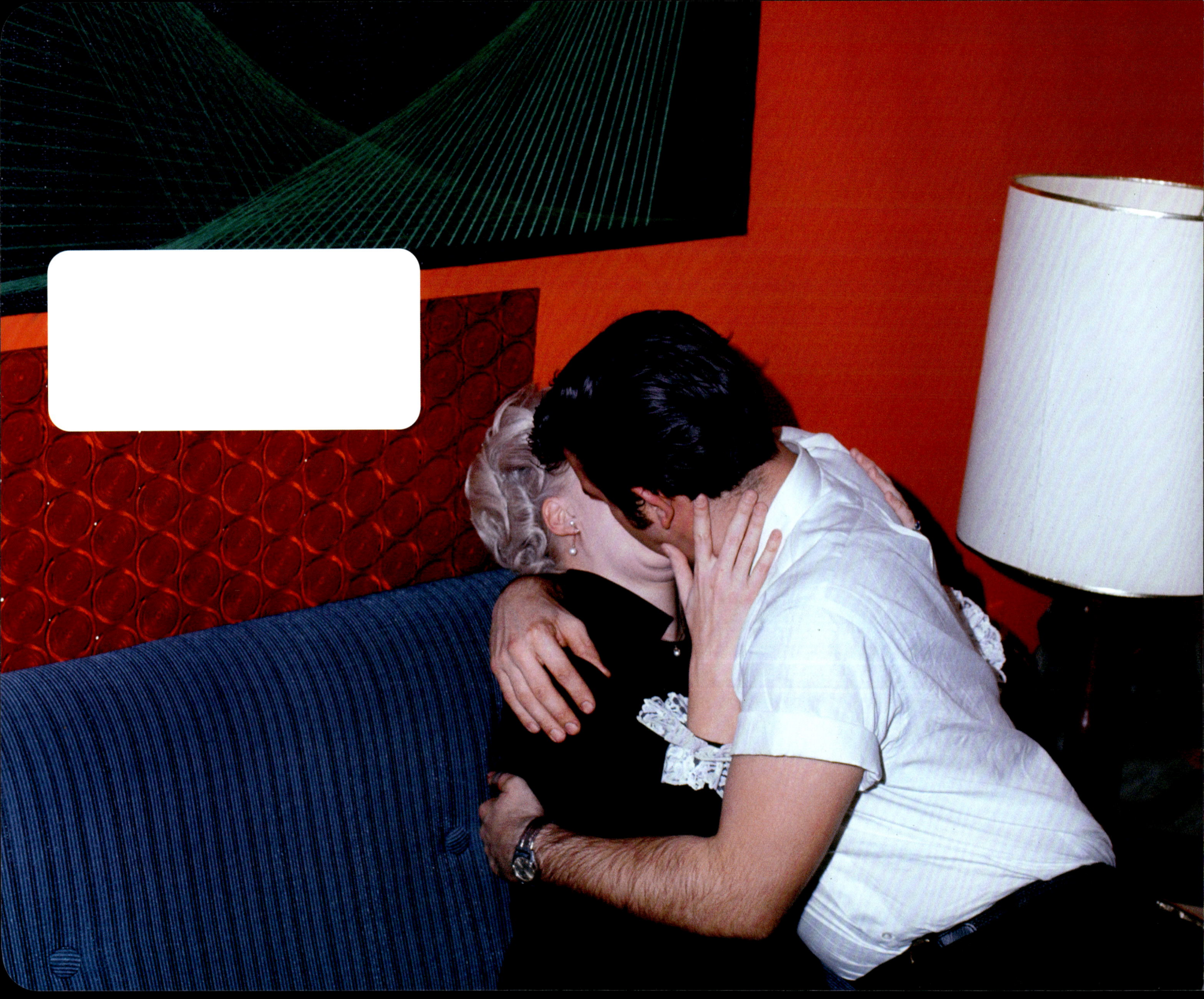

KEEP YOUR
OPINION TO
YOURSELF.

BE THE CHANGE
YOU WANT TO SEE

NOW IS A
GOOD TIME

CHAOS MAKE
THE MUSE

YOU DON'T
KNOW ME

THIS WORLD
MAKES ME
SICK.

I WILL GROW
UP LATER.

NO INSPIRATION
TODAY
SORRY

FUCK YOU!
I DID MY BEST

CREATE
EVERY DAY

MOVE BITCH!

NEVER
WORK!

WHAT A PERFECT WASTE OF TIME

I NEED SEROTONIN

DREAM BIG FART loud

KEEP TALKING I'M DIAGNOSING YOU.

REMEMBER KISSING

I look BETTER IN THE NUDE

ALWAYS SMELL IT FIRST

PUMP UP THE VALIUM

HOW TO DISAPPEAR?

DATING TIPS: DON'T

NO TIME FOR YOUR BULL SHIT

I'M MAKING PROGRESS

WHO WANTS TO FUCKING PARTY?

ANOTHER COFFEE?

SORRY FOR HAVING GREAT TITS AND CORRECT OPINIONS

LOVE YOURSELF NOT ME

TOURISTS GO HOME!

HELLO, I'D LIKE A DRINK!

NOT SAD BUT NOT HAPPY

YESTERDAY YOU SAID TOMORROW

MAYBE I'M HAPPY BUT ASYMPTOMATIC

POPULARITY IS FOR STUPID PEOPLE.

I THINK I THINK TOO MUCH

I'M NOT ENTIRELY HERE

I WISH I HAD MORE MIDDLE FINGERS

I'll BE BACK IN FIVE MINUTES.

I TOLD MY THERAPIST ABOUT YOU

KEEP YOUR OPINION TO YOURSELF

STOP STARING AT MY TITS

AM I SELF CENTERED OR IS IT JUST ME?

YOU CALL THAT ERECT?

WHY NOT?

DON'T LET ANYONE ELSE RUIN YOUR DAY, RUIN IT YOURSELF.

I'M IN MY: "I DON'T CARE" ERA.

ZZZZZ ...

GO BACK TO BED

I HATE
EVERYONE

I ♡
FRANK
OCEAN

HOPELESS
ROMANTIC

I KNOW I'M
YOUR FAVORITE

I LIKE
MEN WITH
BRAINS

TALENTS :
SLEEPING

CUTE BUT
OVERTHINKER

TOO BUSY
FOR BULLSHIT

WHAT THE FUCK
IS REALLY
GOING ON ?

I LOVE TO
MAKE BOYS CRY

ME PRETENDING
EVERYTHING IS OK

EAT PUSSY
ITS ORGANIC.

SMALL BOOBS BIG DREAMS	I NEED A BREAK.	FUCK LOVE GET MONEY
CUTE BUT SCORPIO	SLOW IS GOOD	YOU HAVE TO KISS ME. IT'S THE LAW.
GOOD SHIT HAPPENS.	CHANGE YOUR PERSPECTIVE	EVOLVE OR DIE
IT TAKES TIME.	EMBRACE THE UNKNOWN	STAY DIFFERENT

SAVE ME
FROM MY MIND

WHAT ARE
YOU WAITING
FOR ?

FORBIDDEN
LUST.

is it WORTH
THE EFFORT?

So WHAT?!

HA! HA! HA!
THE EARTH IS IN
CHAOS.

HoLD ME CLOSER
TINY BASTARD

YES MOM
TOOK ACID

YOU'RE DOING
GREAT

LiFE iS NOT
A RACE

I'M NICER
WHEN I LiKE
MY OUTFIT

FRIENDS ARE
FAMiLY TOO

I HATE
EXPLAINING
SHIT.

I'M SAD
I NEED MONEY.

I MISS
MY ENERGY

DO IT
ANYWAY

PLEASE
RELAX

WHAT IS
NORMAL?

BE YOURSELF.

WORK IS
SHIT

JOYFULLY
SUBVERSIVE

GO FASCINATE
SOMEONE ELSE

DON'T
GET SICK

THIS IS WHAT
A FEMINIST
lOOKS LIKE

WHATEVER!

KEEP YOUR lAWS OFF MY BODY

PROUD MOM

MAKE OUT NOT WAR

FREE HUGS

STAND UP SPEAK UP FIGHT BACK

LIFE IS SEXUALLY TRANSMITTED

THE OBVIOUS ESCAPES MANY

WILL ACCEPT MERCY FUCK

RACE MIXING IS cool

lOST IN SPACE

I DON'T UNDERSTAND WHAT I'M SAYING

I MAKE
BOYS CRY

BORN VIRGIN
AGAIN

HAPPY

FORGET IT

WEIRDO

YOUR COMPUTER
NEED TO RESTART

is YOUR HAIR
JUST KIDDING?

NOT YOUR
BITCH

WANT KID?
TAKE MINE

NO REGRETS

AND SO WHAT
IF I AM?

DOES IT
BOTHER YOU
THAT I'M FABULOUS?

COULDN'T CARE
LESS

EDITORIAL DIRECTION
DAVID DESRIMAIS

ART DIRECTION AND DESIGN
AGNÈS DAHAN STUDIO
AGNÈS DAHAN AND RAPHAËLLE PICQUET

EDITED BY
LEE SHULMAN

WORDS BY
THOMAS LÉLU

ON AN INITIATIVE OF
THE ANONYMOUS PROJECT

© JBE BOOKS, 2025
ISBN: 978-2-36568-112-4
LEGAL DEPOSIT: JUNE 2025
PRINTED IN CHINA

JBE BOOKS
90 RUE DE LA FOLIE-MÉRICOURT
75011 PARIS, FRANCE

JBE-BOOKS.COM